LEARN HOW TO :

IN TODAY'S FOST   ⌐LIMATE

A GUIDE TO
FOSTER PARENTING;
EVERYTHING BUT THE KIDS!

Mary Ann Goodearle, MS

TRAFFORD

• Canada • UK • Ireland • USA •

Note for Librarians: A cataloguing record for this book is available from Library and
Archives Canada at www.collectionscanada.ca/amicus/index-e.html
ISBN 1-4120-7847-4

Offices in Canada, USA, Ireland and UK
This book was published *on-demand* in cooperation with Trafford Publishing.
On-demand publishing is a unique process and service of making a book available for
retail sale to the public taking advantage of on-demand manufacturing and Internet
marketing. On-demand publishing includes promotions, retail sales, manufacturing,
order fulfilment, accounting and collecting royalties on behalf of the author.

Book sales for North America and international:
Trafford Publishing, 6E–2333 Government St.,
Victoria, BC v8t 4p4 CANADA
phone 250 383 6864 (toll-free 1 888 232 4444)
fax 250 383 6804; email to orders@trafford.com
Book sales in Europe:
Trafford Publishing (uk) Limited, 9 Park End Street, 2nd Floor
Oxford, UK ox1 1hh UNITED KINGDOM
phone 44 (0)1865 722 113 (local rate 0845 230 9601)
facsimile 44 (0)1865 722 868; info.uk@trafford.com
Order online at:
trafford.com/05-2745

10 9 8 7 6 5 4 3 2

Acknowledgements

I would like to thank all of the foster and adoptive parents that I have had the privilege to know and work with. You have inspired me to put together the information in this book that will help all foster parents survive in the foster care system. You all know as I do, that taking care of foster children is only half of the job! I appreciate the work you do and I want to enable more people to join in your vocation to be there for kids in the future.

I appreciate the patience and support from my husband, Allen. Without his love and encouragement, I would have been in this adventure alone. He has contributed great stories and examples from his own childhood and foster care experiences. They are priceless to me and I hope the readers love his contributions as much as I do! He is my best friend and partner in work and life.

Thanks to Bobbie Bruehl, my granddaughter, the little girl on the cover. Special thanks to Breanna Bruehl, another granddaughter, for her assistance with proof-reading. She is a very sharp girl and will probably write her own book one day.

To Kristine and Scott, my biological kids, who are in their thirties and have their own families. Thanks for letting me talk about you guys. I know it got personal and I appreciate you both for allowing me to share our stories. Love you both!

My adopted children, John, Brenna, Jane, Chcyenne, Jake, Jared and Jamie are all in my heart regardless of where some of them are today. To Jake, Jared and Jamie, you gave me lots of examples to talk about! You guys are all very special to me. Thank you for letting me be your mom. Thank you too, to all of the foster children who shared their lives with us, even if it was only for a short time! Melissa, I'm proud of you!

I also want thank my friend, Barbara Liener for her love and encouragement. Finally special thanks my brother, Joe Pompa and wife, Paula for allowing me to share their story of foster care and adoption. Love you guys!

Contents

Introduction

Welcome to the unique and challenging world of foster care. If you are just entering this profession, you probably have not yet realized some of the challenges you are about to encounter. Foster parenting is kind of like your first trip to Disney Land. You have an idea in your mind what it will be like, but until you actually experience this new world, you are in for some surprises! If you are already foster parenting, you have an idea of what twists and turns lay ahead. Don't worry if the ride becomes too rough because help is on the way.

My primary goal and theme throughout this book is to help foster parents improve the climate in which they work and live. I want to help create better environments for fostering couples and singles in which to survive and continue helping foster children for a long time to come. Too many people get excited about becoming foster parents only to get a bad taste of it and quit. The majority of foster care agencies experience huge turnovers in foster parents. Historically agencies have dealt with this problem by recruiting more foster parents, who in turn, become frustrated and quit too. I know many foster parents who feel that they are dispensable commodities to their foster care agencies!

I will be exploring the reasons for foster parents' disillusionments and assisting you in how to overcome some of the obstacles to long-term success. Children need loving and dedicated foster parents. My hope is that you will stick around and be there for them for a long time. We are going to begin a journey together to try and make your vocation as a foster parent a long and rewarding experience.

The foster care system itself, outside of parenting the foster children, is much more difficult to survive in than you might have expected. There are many factors that contribute to the challenge of surviving in the system. Unfortunately, parenting children is only half of the battle. I think this fact may come as a great surprise to many new foster parents.

There are lots of books, trainings, and people available to give you advice on how to parent children with difficult behaviors. Although I too am one of those resources, I also recognize that foster parents need more than just that kind of help. Most of us understand that foster children have challenging behaviors and emotional difficulties. As a foster parent, you can never get enough training in dealing with the kids. After many years as a foster and adoptive parent, I still learn new methods for managing children's behaviors. Yet, that kind of knowledge is not enough to insure survival as a foster parent!

Have you ever received any help or training on how to survive the foster care system? Foster parents need a lot more than good parenting skills. Here, we are going to be looking at ways to strengthen your survival skills while living and working within the foster care system.

Working in the foster care and the social services systems is as equally challenging as parenting the foster children.

You will be requiring much more than good parenting skills to achieve longevity and success in today's foster care climate.

Most people enter into foster care with altruistic motives. They have the desire to provide loving homes for children in need. They want to help kids succeed in life. In fact, surveys prove this. In a survey I conducted in 1995 among the foster parents I queried, the number one answer to the question, "Why did you become a foster parent?" was "To provide love and help for needy children." Seventy-nine percent of the foster parents fell into that category. The answer that came in second was "I want to help a child improve."

People's motivations for becoming foster parents help explain why so many foster parents become burned out and quit too soon. Whatever your personal reasons are for wanting to become a foster parent, please understand that altruistic motives are great. They are an absolute pre-requisite for the job. You need to have a big heart and the desire to help kids. You will not survive long without that. But, you also need to learn how to survive in the foster care system itself!

In addition, if you are becoming a foster parent wanting to help children and needing to see them change and improve their circumstances, you might be in for a big let down. Most kids in foster care return to their biological homes. Unfortunately, foster parents don't always view that end as a success. Their own view of success would be to have their foster children permanently removed from bad environments. Many foster parents feel they have failed their foster children when they allow the foster care system to return children to their biological homes. They most often feel powerless in that process.

A child's stay in your home may be brief or lengthy. You have to be able to settle for whatever you are able to offer your foster child during that time. In addition, you will feel as though you have very limited control over the decision to return your child to his former situation. It is very painful and worrisome for foster parents when their foster children go back home, especially if the foster parents don't see that home as being ready to care for the child.

When comparing what you have to offer a child in your home to what you perceive the biological parents have to offer, in your own mind you will have no question which home would be better for your foster child. It is very hard to stand by and watch things happen in situations where you feel that you have little control over the outcomes.

To make all of this more survivable for you, you will need to develop a realistic approach to this profession. First, you are taking over parenting children who come from families that have been very chaotic for a very long time. The children's challenging behaviors and the walls they build around themselves didn't materialize overnight. Second, their biological parents are not going to magically become the parents you would like to see them become, nor is the system looking for them to be anywhere near perfect in order to get their children back. Third, the system is not going to be there for you in every way you might have expected. I will have a whole chapter dedicated to avoiding and/or surviving foster parent abuse allegations with more about that later.

Now, if this is all starting to sound a little negative, I apologize. My intent is not to scare you away. I want to prepare you for the reality of what is to come. If you are a seasoned foster parent, you probably have worked through some of this stuff already. But, no matter how long you have been around, there are going to be some things that are hard to digest at times. I want to assist you in developing an approach to this job of foster parenting, where you will be able to have realistic expectations that allow you to survive in this system for the long run.

While most of you have the altruistic motives in your

hearts, I want to put survival skills on your foster parenting resumes. Most of you wouldn't be here if you weren't trying to help kids, but many of you won't be there for them in the future if you don't become savvy about surviving in the foster care system!

There you have in a nutshell what this book is all about. You have got to become a professional! Foster parenting is not a hobby. It is not for amateurs. While it is possible to learn on the job, foster parents today, need to take a more aggressive course of education for themselves. To make any kind of sense of how the system works and why social workers and judges do what they do, foster parents need to take a crash course in survival as professionals in a world that most of them have not been privy to in the past. That is where this book will help you.

My husband, Allen, and I have fostered over 45 children in the past ten years. We adopted 7 of them, all with the label of "severely emotionally disturbed." Allen is a former foster child himself. He is an adult survivor of 14 different foster homes. I will be sharing some of his stories and points of view along with some of our experiences working in the foster care and adoption systems. I am a former child protection social worker, foster care program coordinator, and state adoption facilitator. I have worked with hundreds of birth parents and foster parents. I will share insights from my work experiences inside the agencies and from mine and Allen's roles as foster and adoptive parents. I have also accumulated a wealth of knowledge from the wonderful foster families I have had the privilege to be associated with in the past. I hope that all of our experiences will assist you to flourish on your journey through foster care, and that you will be there for children who need you for many more years to come.

This book doesn't necessarily have to be read from cover to cover. I have set the chapters up by topic. Although I would like you to read and reread the entire contents, for those of you who are either too busy to sit down and read the whole thing, or for those of you who do not like to read whole books, I organized the material here in chapters that you may pick and choose what is of interest and of most importance to you. You may find yourself not needing a certain topic now, but might have to return to this book for reference later when the need arises.

Allen and I are touring the country and speaking to foster parents everywhere. We are sharing our story and the stories of many other foster parents in order to help develop a better climate for foster parents in which to survive and thrive. If you have a foster care or adoption story you would like us to share, you can contact us through our website at www.fostercare-trainer.com or email us at newparadigms2000@yahoo.com. If you would like us to appear at a workshop or conference in your area, either e-mail or call us at 497-243-0677. You may also contact us by mail at: New Paradigms Unlimited, 5363 Hwy 8 East, Mena Arkansas, 71953. We welcome your concerns and comments. Most of all, we wish you Godspeed in your journey through foster care!

Chapter

1

PROFESSIONALISM

We come together in this profession of foster parenting from many different backgrounds, professions and interests. Most of us are married couples, but foster care in most states has been opened up to single folks as well. Some of us are full-time parents while others of us hold down full-time jobs while parenting. Even though we are individually each very different, we have one great common mission. That is simply to open our homes and hearts to children in need. Most of us don't really know what to expect when we first become foster parents, but we do know that kids out there need our assistance.

For Allen and me, even with the benefit of my working inside of a foster care agency, the job of foster parenting was much more difficult than we had ever imagined. That was a big surprise to me. I thought, as a social worker, I knew how foster parents felt! Until I became a foster parent myself, I worked with foster parents everyday without truly appreciating what a difficult job they had!

Living the role of foster parent was far more challenging than I had ever imagined. I'm sure that a large number of other foster parents have felt that way too. Knowing how much harder the job would be with my experience as a social worker, I knew it would be even more of a challenge to other folks who didn't have the added benefit of working inside a foster care agency. I hope that by reading some of my experiences, you will be better equipped to weather some of the surprises and storms on your own horizon.

I want to tell you what it was like for us when we first started out foster parenting. We had a tremendous advantage over most people who are just starting out in this field. I was a child protection social worker in a large county program. In addition to that, Allen is a former foster child. We both had more exposure to the foster care world than most people have experienced. But, even with all our knowledge of the system, little did we realize that we were in for some big awakenings.

Like most other people do in this profession, we started out wanting to help kids. With Allen having been a troubled teenager at one time himself, we thought we would be in a good position to work with teenage boys. Allen's inside knowledge of how adolescent boys think was truly helpful, and still is today. We were licensed by a private treatment foster care agency in Wisconsin. All of the children and teens that came through that agency were kids who couldn't qualify for regular foster homes because of their severe challenging behaviors. Some of them had already been in foster homes that asked to have them removed.

I always joke about wanting to hear the pitter patter of little feet around the house again. Both of our biological children, Scott and Kristine, were married and on their own a couple of years already before we began foster parenting. So, we had our empty nest syndrome and wanted kids in our lives again. Like many other people, we only thought about what it was going to be like caring for the foster children. We were exited about getting our first placement and taking care of a child without the realization that there would be a lot more expected from us.

When our first child arrived, the pitter patter of little feet turned out to be the pitter patter of really big feet. Size 13 to be exact. Our first foster son, Brad, was 15 years old and over 6 feet tall. He had flaming red hair and a flaming hot temper to match it. In some ways he was like a big 5 year -old.

Along with all of his possessions and emotional baggage came something I wasn't prepared for. He brought with him a whole entourage of people who soon became involved in our lives. As a case worker who was working with foster parents, I had no idea the impact all of those people would have on us. In addition to getting used to Brad in our lives, we had Brad's single mother, his social worker, his therapist and his special education teachers as new additions to our weekly routine. (Not to mention law enforcement officers and the judicial system that followed shortly.)

I had observed other foster families experience all of these new people in their lives, and thought it was no big deal until they were all in mine! Home life as I had previously known it no longer existed. It was as if we were dropped into an aquarium with all of these people on the outside looking in at us. Our private family life was no longer our own. Our normal routines and plans were subject to approval by everyone.

Brad's mom had weekly visits for Sunday afternoons, so we had to make sure we were home for her to pick him up and drop him off. But she never just dropped him off. She usually came inside and told us about all the trouble she had with him, while his four year old brother ripped around terrorizing our house. We were happy to listen to her and offer advice, but it became very time consuming and draining.

Our social worker from the agency came on Wednesdays, an hour before Brad got home from school. I was at work at the county during the start of these visits, but when I got home she was usually still there. She would talk to Allen about how Brad was doing and then spend another hour with Brad when he got home.

On Thursday evenings, Brad went to our neighboring county to see his therapist. That usually started at 5 PM and got Allen and Brad home around 7 PM. Brad was usually in a foul mood after those visits, as he also was after his social worker's visits, and after being dropped off by his mom on Sundays. That made it a minimum of three nights of foul moods each week!

We were real gluttons for punishment because within a month of Brad's placement with us, 16 year-old Rick came along. With him he brought along his entourage of people too, so the number of outside people involved in our lives instantly doubled!

Without going into more details about what our daily scheduled entailed, let me just simply tell you that dealing with all of these people was as equally hard as parenting the two boys. We had decided that I would keep working full time (I figured that was the easiest for me!) and Allen would be the fulltime parent, chauffer, counselor, bouncer, and whatever else was required of him.

What I quickly came to better understand and deeply appreciate was the work all of the foster parents in my program did. They didn't simply parent needy kids! That, as I soon discovered for myself, was only half of their jobs. Believe me when I say this. Most of the social workers, without having the actual hands on experience of having foster children in their own homes, have no idea how tough the job of foster parenting is!

No matter how many times the social workers hear from you about your difficult situations and trials as a foster parent, unless they have actually walked in your shoes, they will never understand how difficult your job is!

Living with the challenging behaviors that foster children bring with them, in itself, is much harder than most agency workers can even begin to imagine. Unless experienced first hand, there is no way to understand how stressful and taxing it can be to live with difficult behaviors 24 hours a day, 7 days a week. That is just the child care part of it. We are here to discuss the rest of the job.

The addition of all these new people to your life and daily routine is a scheduling challenge at the very least! In addition to making the time for them, they come to you with a vast array of opinions and advice about what you should and should not be doing as far as parenting their child clients. Not having to live with the children themselves, they have no idea of how the actual application of their treatment plans affects the foster families.

For example, I used to tell foster parents to treat their foster children just as if they were they own children. The actual application of that advice could never work. Foster kids have different and more challenging behaviors than most of our own kids. They also do not belong to us. There are as many reasons to treat them differently as there are reasons to treat them the same. I didn't know how far off I was on that advice until I became a foster parent myself!

Unfortunately, many of the child protection social workers and case workers for foster families in our program were fresh out of college with little hands-on experience in parenting even their own children. Many of them were still single or newly married. Even if they had children of their own, it in no way prepared them for what the job of foster parenting entailed.

MOST SOCIAL WORKERS AND CASE WORKERS DON'T UNDERSTAND THE DIFFICULTY OF YOUR JOB AS A FOSTER PARENT!

On the other hand, as foster parents, we haven't walked in their shoes either. Social workers have a huge amount of responsibility and usually not enough time to handle the amount of crises that arise during the course of each day. Much of their time is spent putting out fires, so to speak.

Here is another shock that I experienced! I didn't realize it at first, but I soon learned that the professionals on our children's cases did not view us as professionals too. Allen and I began to feel as though many things were dictated to us without explanation or consideration for our feelings and plans. Many times we waited days for return phone calls from the Departments of Human Services when we had questions to ask them that felt urgent to us at the time.

Considering that I was shocked and surprised as a social worker myself at how difficult it was to be at the receiving end of social services, it left no doubt in my mind that my colleagues in social work also did not understand how the foster parents felt when experiencing all of these changes in their lives!

Shortly after becoming foster parents, my job at the agency changed. I applied for director of the foster care program. (This was a different agency than the one we were licensed as foster parents by.) My new job was recruiting, training, licensing and supporting foster parents. I was fortunate to have a completely new view of the other side of foster care; the side the rest of the case workers could never imagine!

I soon began to hear a resounding statement from the foster parents in my program:

"The social workers need to walk in our shoes for awhile."

As part of my thesis for my graduate degree, I conducted a survey with former foster parents from my agency. The results revealed that nearly 50% of the former foster parents rated 'Stress on my family,' as the number one reason they had left our program. They felt strongly that the social workers didn't have an understanding of the difficulty of foster parenting and the impact felt by their families. Many of the foster parents felt that the social workers should have been required to be foster parents for one month before they were allowed to be case managers!

It bothered most of the foster parents that the majority of their case workers were newly out of college, rookies in foster care so to speak. Not only did they lack experience in social work, they had no parenting experience other than growing up in families. Their families of origin were the opposite end of the spectrum from the families they case managed. Their own families were able to send them to college and support them during the process. They had no exposure to the world of abuse, neglect, and foster care.

The foster parents felt under-valued and dispensable. They did not feel as though they were treated as professionals by the rest of the foster care treatment team!

The professionals who looked at foster parents as not be-

ing professionals had less exposure to parenting challenging children than the foster parents had!

As we have begun to see, the job of foster parent is absolutely unique. It is very hard for anyone else who is not a foster parent to comprehend. As foster parents, we are as much professionals as the other professionals we work with on the team. We have to start viewing ourselves as professionals and gain that level of recognition from the rest of the foster care treatment team members!

Foster parents and social workers have many things in common. But, I would like to have you think about the special qualifications and requirements that are unique to foster parents and that are vastly different from the social workers and other professionals involved on the case. Let's take a closer look:

- Everyone involved in the foster care treatment plan has a job to do requiring education and competencies unique to a given position. The social workers, psychologists, teachers, etc. all have job descriptions in their contracts. They have performance reviews related to those job descriptions. Performance expectations are spelled out for them in black and white. It is required as part of a social worker's license or practice to undergo review meetings and annual training requirements. Supervisors and other professionals are on board to help provide guidance. When compared to foster parents, there are huge differences. For them there are expectations for performance without clear job descriptions, professional training or career guidance. Many foster parents have felt left out on the line to dry all by themselves. Even worse, many programs are facing budget cuts which usually eliminate foster parent training before cuts to the other staff member's training.

This past year, Allen and I had the honor of speaking at a well known National Foster Parent's Conference. We conducted two workshops there. When we asked for a show of hands of how many foster parents were in the audience, out of around fifty people in each workshop, only two or three people in each group were foster parents. The rest of the participants were agency staff! Where were all the foster parents at the 'NATIONAL FOSTER PARENTS' CONFERENCE?' The funding obviously wasn't there for them. Agencies are willing to send their own staff to trainings at the cost of $350 plus hotels and travel, but foster parents are usually left on their own to attend. Few foster parents have the resources to attend training and pay for a babysitter while they are away. Finding a babysitter who is qualified and willing to take care of foster kids is another whole challenge!

• Another obvious area of difference is that foster parenting is a 24 hour a day, 7 days per week job. I'm sure you know that. But have you considered how different that is from the rest of the professionals' jobs? As a foster parent you live at your workplace. Your are surrounded by work related problems and stress while you are at home, and for most foster parents that is after they have already worked at their other jobs for eight or more hours a day. The other professionals don't literally take their work home with them. While your job has considerable affects on the rest of your family, the other professionals work has no bearing on their loved ones except for maybe dinner conversation or "bring your daughter to work day." They get to go home after work. You live at your work!

- The other professionals don't have the same level of emotional vulnerability that is inherent in your role as a foster parent. The social worker may become attached to the child clients, but you and your family grow to love your foster child. You laugh, cry and live your daily lives with your foster child. In most ways you treat him as if he were your own. The entire case outcome affects you and your entire family on a higher level than it does with the other professionals. When a child leaves your home to return to his birth family, whether it is good or bad for him, you and your family are profoundly affected. Most likely, you feel a sense of loss. Your social worker sees the child returning to his birth parents as achieving the goal of the case plan. Social workers may not understand why it is so hard for you to let go. Most agencies don't even provide follow-up information to foster parents about how well their former foster child is doing. In fact, where I worked it was totally against the agency's policy. Fortunately the powers that be at the agencies are beginning to realize that it is better for everyone involved to be informed and stay involved when appropriate. Kids need to keep all positive influential adults in their lives, not to mention that continued contact of some sort helps foster parents to cope with their feelings of loss and worry, and to be more able to move on and help more children.

- All of the professionals involved with the case know every intimate detail of your life. It's true. Remember the licensing interviews and perhaps writing your biography for the agency? Most foster parents are asked to bare their soles. All of that becomes a part of the record and licensing information in a file about you. The file is available to any agency worker who wants to know what your family is all about. On the other side of the coin, you don't know anything about the personal lives of the professionals you work with on the case. Most social workers have been trained to not give out personal information to their clients and families with whom they work. In addition to the original foster home study being in your file, the weekly events or crises that arise under your roof are a matter of record too. All of this information is closely scrutinized by the case worker and subjective to how each social worker interprets it. What do you know about your social worker?

• Good or even great qualities about you that would be considered admirable among humans on this planet can be judged by your social worker or agency as not conducive to good foster parent material. Most of us admire people who ask questions, challenge the status quo, and try to make the world a better place to live. If you do that as a foster parent, you are judged by some of the professionals as opinionated, demanding or resistive. Some social workers expect completely compliant foster parents. One of the best foster parents I ever worked with asked lots of questions, volunteered her opinions, and made her feelings known. My co-workers didn't like using that foster home because they viewed her as difficult to work with. But at the same time, she took very challenging children and did an excellent job with them. She was intelligent, nurturing, and patient. Listening to her and considering her opinions seemed to me like the natural thing to do. Some of my co-workers didn't want to deal with that. The moral of this story is: You can be an above average person and foster parent, but not be recognized as that by the other professionals. It can, in fact, be the complete opposite! We expect the professionals to have opinions, question the status quo, possess intelligence, and do what they think is right. If foster parents have these qualities, they are viewed as hostile or opinionated by some social workers.

- If things go a little astray for foster parents, they get blame and scrutiny. They can easily become the focus of agency or criminal investigations. A child making a false accusation can spin a foster parent's life into instant turmoil. When this happens, foster parents have no where to turn for help and support. (We'll have a whole chapter devoted to this later.) For decades social workers have been trained to believe what children tell them because children don't lie. Fortunately that kind of thinking is beginning to change, but there is still a lot of it out there. Foster parents can become suspects very easily. The credibility they think they have with the agency may fly out the window when any kind of trouble arises. My husband and I have been the victims of this kind of thinking. (More about that later.) The other professionals can all turn to each other when crises arise. Their credibility is usually not challenged or questioned. They receive the support and advice of their peers and their administrators. Foster parents are out there alone when certain troubles arise!

- Foster parents get paid a stipend, usually minimal, for their foster children. The money is intended to help them break even in supporting additional children, though most times, they end up supplementing this allowance with their own funds. Events such as proms, class trips, and normal family entertainment strain foster parent's budgets. My husband and I took four kids to the movie theater in Fort Lauderdale. Between the tickets to get in and refreshments, we spent over $80.00. Adding a few extra kids to the most common events like movies or dining out becomes close to undoable for most families. Then consider that some kids come into foster care without even possessing the bare necessities such as jackets or calculators for school. Most agencies offer a clothing allowance at the beginning of a placement. In agencies I have worked with, that is usually around $100.00 per child. Now days that doesn't go very far, especially when it comes to buying the big necessities such as jackets or winter clothes. Think about what you might have to spend at the beginning of each new school year on clothing and school supplies for two or three extra children! That stipend doesn't go very far. In spite of this, I still have heard social workers and others say things such as, "they must be doing it for the money." Even if a foster parent is receiving $1000.00 per month for a difficult child, it doesn't break down to very much per hour. When you calculate that amount into dollars per hour for watching and dealing with delinquent or defiant behavior 24 hours a day for 30 days, it translates to pennies per hour. Now consider this. Social workers are not among the highest paid professionals either, but have you ever heard a foster parent say, "The social workers are doing it for the money?" Do foster parents even begin to question anything about what social workers are paid and how they spend their money? There is obviously an enormous difference on how financial compensation is viewed between social workers and foster parents!

- In addition to working 24 hours a day, foster parents cannot leave their foster children with just any babysitter. In my old agency, care providers for foster children had to undergo criminal background checks. They had to be over 18 years old, and possess above average child care skills. The point is that you could not hire your 17 year-old neighbor girl to baby-sit for $2.50 per hour like other normal parents usually can do. Allen and I had to look far and wide for adults who were willing to care for our foster children. They had to be willing to undergo the agency background check, receive training, and work for an amount that would fit into our budget. Foster parents lose all of the spontaneity that other people enjoy when it comes to simply leaving their children in someone else's care. Foster parents' much needed time away from their kids, at the very least, has to be well planned out in advance and subject to finding agency accredible and affordable help! We know how hard that is, but the social workers do not understand this.

By looking at some of these differences between the roles of foster parents and the roles of the other professionals, it becomes quite clear that foster parenting is challenging, unique, undervalued, and misunderstood. Professionalizing the work of foster parents must be the foundation to the future success of our foster care programs.

Foster parents, individually, must think of themselves as professionals, and as a larger group, they must work togeth-

er to gain professional credibility and recognition from their professional peers and administrators!

The dictionary defines professional as: 1) An occupation requiring training or specialized study. 2) The body of qualified persons in an occupation or field.

Would you consider foster parents as a body of qualified persons in an occupation or field? Of course you would! The Rodale Synonym Finder provides these synonyms for professional: efficient, competent, specialist, veteran, trained, skillful. Foster parents are all of that! If persons applying for foster care licenses were not trained and competent, they wouldn't get their licenses. Think about the process you went through in the beginning. It probably included personal references, professional references, background checks, credit checks, and a compete autobiography you were required to write. Your agency acquired more information about you than it is even legal to ask for in any other job applicants! (Such as age, race, marital status, religious affiliation, sexual orientation and so on and so on.)

In addition to knowing you very well, most agencies now require pre-service training. My agency required 24 hours of training prior to licensing and an additional 24 hours each year. People (myself included) are making professions out of training foster parents. If you surf the web, you'll find hundreds of sites offering training for foster and adoptive parents. There are free newsletters, conferences, books, and e-magazines that are all dedicated to training foster parents. You will also find chat rooms and support groups. One that I ran across was a support group for foster parents who have been falsely accused of abusing their foster child. Local groups of foster parents are organizing to form chapters of support groups. It is great to see this happening outside of the agency's domain. Many agencies offer support groups that are facilitated by their own staff. Now there are groups at the city, state and national levels that are not affiliated with any child placement or case supervising agencies. Does all of this sound like professionals organizing? It is a great beginning.

As a body, foster parents are starting to unite. The responsibilities intrinsic to foster parenting give great credence to the need for banning together. Foster parents are entrusted with the very little human beings that the foster care system is striving to protect. It seems to me that the position of foster parent would require the highest level of a professional! Foster parents report the progress of the biological parent visits, school performance, emotional behavior, health and so much more. Could all that responsibility be entrusted to a non-professional. I say not!

In my survey of foster parents, I asked the questions: "Do you feel as though you are treated like a professional person by your agency?" and "How important is it to you to be treated as a professional by your agency?" The foster parents almost unanimously felt that being treated as a professional was very important to them, but sixty seven percent responded that they were not treated as professionals. During a debriefing session held at the end of my survey, the foster parents stated that they felt they were at the bottom of the totem pole where rank and status were concerned. Many of them said that they felt as though their opinions and ideas didn't count.

Having worked among child protection and foster care social workers, I found that there is no middle ground in how they think of foster parents. In fact, most of their opinions fell at opposite ends of the spectrum. Some of them placed high esteem on the foster parents while others looked at them as glorified babysitters. My co-workers made two kinds of statements to me that demonstrated how they felt toward foster parents. They either said, "You must be a saint to be a foster parent" or they said, "You have to be crazy to be a foster parent." The extremes in thinking that were going on in my agency appear to be prevalent in the larger foster care community as well. Personally, I don't feel completely crazy yet, nor do I even begin to think of myself as a saint. As a foster parent, I would like to think of myself as a professional and at another level I would like to feel as though I am a member of a professional group.

Diagram 1-a demonstrates how the foster parents view themselves in the scheme of things.

Diagram 1-b demonstarates the ideal foster cae treatment team.

1a. The Reality (As foster parents see it.)

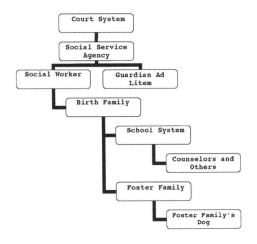

1b. The Ideal (The way we'd like to see it!)

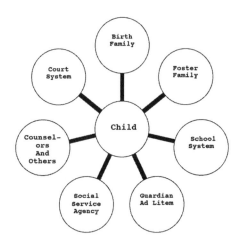

You can clearly see that in diagram 1a, the foster parents view themselves at the bottom of the heap of professionals. In diagram 1b, the foster child, who is receiving everyone's services, is at the center. Everyone else is equally contributing to that child's needs. That is the ideal that we should all be working toward.

In order for positive change to take place, the playing field between foster parents and other foster care personnel must be leveled. You can be sure that the other professional members of the foster care system are not going to run out and level it for us. It is up to each individual to take the necessary steps to professionalize the work of foster parenting. Change does not come swift or easy. In the meantime, foster parents must commit to succeeding in an imperfect system while making incremental changes that are within their power to achieve. I don't know of any systems that are perfect anyway. We live in a universe that is far from perfect. Most of us manage to thrive in spite of imperfections.

The following are some steps that foster parents can take in order to start making changes toward professionalism both for themselves and for the entire foster parenting group as a whole:

1) **Always think of yourself as a professional.** If you were an engineer or a math teacher, you would identify your profession by what you do. As a foster parent you raise and care for other people's children. You are trained and licensed for this and high expectations for job performance are imposed upon you. You are a professional parent. Think, act, walk, and talk like a professional. Don't be intimidated or in awe of the other professionals. You are one of them and are entitled to the same status!

2) **Continue to learn and seek out new information that will improve your skills.** If your agency doesn't offer the kind of training you think you need, seek it out for yourself. You are the best judge of which areas you need to improve in your work.

   a) There are numerous local, state and national foster care trainings and conferences you could attend that offer a wide variety of workshop topics. Take a mini-vacation away from the kids and go! In addition to learning, you will enjoy the company of many others who are doing the same kind of work you do.

   b) Become a library or bookstore groupie. One of my favorite one hour get-a-ways is to mull over interesting professional books at Barnes and Nobles, while drinking a Starbuck's coffee. At the end of this book there will be websites that offer training for foster and adoptive parents and some books that I recommend you read. You can get inexpensive training without ever leaving your house!

c) Another way to learn more about your foster parenting profession is to seek out a mentor for yourself. Look within your own community of foster parents. Who do you think is doing a great job? How do you think that person manages to survive in the system? How can you be more like him or her? What ideas do you have to share? As stated by Oliver Goldsmith, "People seldom improve when they have no other model but themselves to copy." Emulate those you admire. If you are fortunate enough to have a good relationship with your social worker, run ideas past her and ask for her input. Learning is a life long process. Look for opportunities everywhere and in everyone. Don't discount anyone because of educational, mental, financial or any other kinds of statuses. You can learn helpful and interesting things from someone you may least expect!

3) **When the going gets tough, don't whine or complain.** Chances are that that whoever you whine or complain to can't or won't help you anyway. Do you know the difference between whining and venting? Venting can be healthy for you, but it becomes whining when you tell it over and over without getting constructive about it. The best way to avoid turning venting into whining is to have a good venting friend. That would be someone you can let it all out to, but

that person will halt you when your venting starts to become whining. After you let it all out, stand back and analyze your feelings and come up with a plan to feel better. If you tend to whine to your agency or your social worker too much, chances are you will get tuned out sooner or later! Worse yet, they may stop giving you placements of new kids because they hate to you whine.

4) **Join a foster parent support group.** If there are none in your area, talk to other foster parents about starting one. Be careful to keep the environment positive. People sometimes whine at support group meetings. Gently and kindly guide the conversation toward constructive problem solving. Sometimes it helps to know that other people feel the same way you do or experience some of the same challenges. You can find ways to problem solve without reinventing the wheel.

Through my and Allen's work training foster parents around the country, we are learning that there are a great number of foster parent support groups who are independent of child placement agencies. Some of them even have paid staff members! One of the major focuses of some of these groups is to bring training in for their local members. That is one of the ways in which Allen and I are able to bring our training workshops around the country.

Also by joining together in support groups, foster parents can have a greater affect on changing the system for the better. Organized support groups can influence law-makers, the media, and child-placement agencies in an effort to professionalize the job of foster parenting and to make things better in the lives of the children we care for.

5) **Remember to always be a team member even if you are not recognized by the others as one.** The treatment team is there for one purpose and that is to treat and protect the children. You have a vital role on this team. (We'll be discussing this in more detail in Chapter 2.) Achieving real team membership and recognition may take some time. Attend meetings on behalf of your child. Don't be afraid to advocate what you think is best for him. Use good judgment as to when it is your turn to contribute. Get people to start listening to you by becoming a good listener to them. Hang in there and show them you are a professional just like them. Sometimes not all of them will act professionally. Remember you are all humans and not always perfect. Maintain your good standards of communication and politeness in spite of how others in the meeting might behave. Read chapter two!

6) **Hold yourself to professional standards.** Set and review your own goals. Revise them and fine tune them when necessary. Going down the wrong road toward a goal that isn't working out will only get you lost somewhere! Be accountable to yourself and set worthy standards. View criticism from your agency or others as a foundation on which to build. Critique yourself. You know better than anyone else what you want to improve and do better.

Definition:

Critique: to be marked by careful evaluation.

   a. Analyze and critique yourself often. Remember that when we criticize others, what we sometimes do, is to project on them our own deep down imperfections.

b. A final word about criticism as stated by Fred Allen, "If criticism had any real power to harm, the skunk would have been extinct by now!" Try to think of that and laugh inside when you are the object of unfriendly criticism. Listen, evaluate and learn. Focus on the job you are doing and how you can do it better.

7) **Learn to recognize your own strengths and limitations.** Know what you can undertake and learn to say "no" to jobs that don't fall within your ability and desire to perform. If placement of a child presents challenges that are beyond the range of what you are equipped or willing to handle, as the late former President Ronald Reagan said, "Just say no." And, say it without guilt or second guessing yourself. Accepting placements that fall outside of your capabilities or willingness only leads to frustration and resentment.

Example: A couple that I am very close to recently accepted placement of a three year old girl who is very emotionally disturbed with severe behavior problems and sexual acting out. They already have a five year old, and a two year old. The addition of this little girl to their home threw the rest of the family into turmoil. Their home became chaotic and barely functional. They told me that their first impression was to say no to this placement based on already having enough on their plates. But, they felt it was their duty to help out the agency. NEVER base your decision to accept or reject a placement on that reason! You cannot be an effective parent when behaviors and challenges get out of your circle of comfort and ability. Perform at your peak, but don't fall off the mountain!

Some foster parents may feel that if they say no to their agency, that the agency will not call them with any new placements. That is far from the truth. You will save everyone lots of work and trouble by saying no when you need to. The agency will call you again. They need you, and most importantly, they need you to not burn out from taking kids who are outside your comfort zone or the safety of your own family. The agency needs you to continue foster parenting and not to quit or burn out because you can't say "No."

8) **Don't ever allow yourself to feel inferior to others on the treatment team.** Whether we are high school graduates or Ph.D.'s, we have all learned from the lessons of life. Don't be intimidated by social workers, doctors, or counselors. Degrees don't make people smarter, they just make them more educated in a particular field! Who can know more about the child you live with than you do? You are the expert on your child. Know that you have lots to offer and be confident in yourself. No matter what the files and paperwork say, you know your child better than anyone else. Think of all the lessons we learned from the movie Forest Gump! Forest didn't hold high degrees in formal education, but his insight into life taught us lessons you can't find in any school or text books. Other people may have knowledge that you don't have, but you know things that they don't know. People with degrees and formal education can learn

from you. Learn from them and teach them what you know.

Here's a funny little story that actually happened to Allen and me many years ago! We owned a used car lot and auto repair shop. One of our customers, who was a college professor, came into our office one day and told us that we didn't charge enough for doing oil changes on cars. He said, "How can you come out just charging $19.95 to change people's oil? It nearly took me all day to change the oil in my car. From now on, I'm bringing it back to you because I just don't have the time to do it." He went on to explain that getting the old oil out of the car was easy enough, but it took him over two hours just to put the new oil into the motor. He complained, "I had to stand there for hours just trying to get that thick goopy oil down that little opening where the dipstick comes out!"

Now for anyone who has never changed oil in a car, that is not where the oil goes in! There is a much simpler method. That is to take off the oil cap and pour in all of the oil in about two minutes or less. So you see, we are not all knowledgeable in everything! Even this PhD. couldn't function outside his own realm of expertise. Don't ever underestimate the value of what you know and the life lessons you have learned!

9) **Keep a journal.** Your case worker documents the progress of your child's case in her file. You should do the same for yourself. Incidents that seem catastrophic one day may be nearly forgotten a week later when you are dealing with foster kids. Behaviors and

observations that are critical to the case go by the wayside if you don't write them down. It happens because there are so many crises with the kids that the details start becoming blurred. I will discuss more about your need to document your child's behaviors in my final chapter, "Surviving Abuse Allegations." For now, suffice it to say that what you write down could help you get out of a jam down the road. Include dates, circumstances, and the facts. Document behaviors and your observations regularly.

In addition to coming in handy when you might get into a jam, documentation serves an even greater purpose for the outcome of your foster child's future. What you write down in your own file might be of critical importance to the case. Behaviors that foster children exhibit after home visits or behaviors that are very unusual will help the decision-makers on the case decide on your child's future. Things you don't write down might have made a difference if you had remembered to share them. Write your own case notes and share them with your social worker.

10) Remember foster care work is not your life! Don't over identify with your profession. At night when your social worker goes home, she is not doing social work there. It is much harder for you as a foster parent to separate professional parenting from who you are because you literally live at your workplace. There are things you can do.

If you have outside interests or hobbies, don't drop or forget about them. Go out for dinner with your significant other and leave the kids at home with a babysitter. Try dating again. (Each other of course!) Ask your foster care agency for respite care. If that is not possible, find another foster family to swap kids once in awhile for couple time alone.

Have mom's hours away while dad takes over for a little while and vice versa. It doesn't have to be so long that the parent who stays home in charge is completely nuts when the other parent gets home.

I'll let you in on my nine o'clock rule. When my husband and I were new foster parents, we parented until we went to bed. We didn't get any time to wind down from the kids. It never failed that as soon as we sat down to relax and read or watch TV someone in the house would say, "I need a bar of soap," or "Can I have a snack," or "I need to borrow your dictionary," and so on and so on all evening long. It used to drive me crazy until I came up with the rule: If you don't have it by 9PM, you don't get it! That way after 9 PM the house was settled down and my husband and I could relax. On school nights the kids stayed up until ten, but they had to be showered and in their own rooms by nine. It wasn't a punishment because their TVs and all their stuff was in their rooms with them. The whole point of the rule was to leave me alone for one hour of the day. I can't tell you how much Allen and I looked forward to nine o'clock! You can have your own version of that rule or make up any others that allow your home to run smoothly and give yourself at least one hour a day of peace and quiet. The bottom line is that you can't be living foster care all 24 hours of the day!

11) **Celebrate your successes big and small!** Foster care is not a financially lucrative venture. Unless you have

completely gone off the deep end, you couldn't be in it for the money. Take time to reflect often on why you are doing it. What is success for you? Will you know it when it comes to you? Are you doing it to help children improve? Improvement for foster kids usually comes slow and sometimes you don't see it when it is actually happening. I used to visit foster homes at least once or twice a month. Much of the time the foster parents thought their foster children hadn't made any improvements. But, in the eyes of someone who only saw the children every 30 days, changes were taking place. It's like watching grass grow. You can't actually see it growing toward the sky, but everyday it keeps growing. On Tuesday you won't notice much difference from Monday, but wait until next Tuesday and you'll surely have to mow it. Celebrate your success. Don't beat yourself up if things don't seem to improve fast enough. Remember, the grass is really still growing and so are the kids!

Furthermore, the success of the case doesn't necessarily depend on what you want for your child. Most often, foster children want to go home to their own parents, even if those parents seem to you like the most horrible people on the face of the planet. Foster kids are comfortable with their own parents. Most foster kids still love them in spite of how they were neglected or mistreated. Their birth homes are familiar to them and their comfort and security strangely rest within that zone. A successful foster care case ends with a safe child. If the birth parent's home is safe, but not as nice as your own home, it can be a tough pill for you to swallow. The success of the case may not necessarily feel good to you!

In that case, celebrate the new life survival skills you taught your foster child. Feel good that you were able to open up a whole new way for your child to think about living. Your foster child will probably go back home and live with his or her birth parents, but because of your love and efforts, your child may be able to see a different kind of future for himself!

On the eve of our 25th wedding anniversary, Allen shared a story with me about one of his experiences in foster care. He was about nine years old and living in a foster home where the whole family was preparing for a party to celebrate the mom and dad's 25th wedding anniversary. Allen was included in the preparations. He said that he never knew anyone who was married that long. He admired that about his foster parents and he made a promise to himself that night. He pledged that if he ever got married, he and his wife would celebrate their own 25th wedding anniversary! He was able to do that. His foster parents, the Ottos, had inspired him. No one in his own family ever stayed married that long. His role model for marriage was his foster parents, and they never knew it!

The morale of the story is that you can celebrate your influence on your foster child's life, whether you know you made a difference or not. Most likely you did!

12) Always maintain the highest level of integrity in everything you do. If you were an accomplished artist you would proudly sign your name on your master-

piece. You can't sign your name on your foster child, but do your job with a level of integrity that you can proudly say, "I did that!" There was a study done by a large firm in Chicago to determine what accounted for the differences between the top producers and the average producers in the company. It was not knowledge, skill or charisma that separated the more successful employees from the less successful. The research team found that the difference between the top and average producers was that the most successful salesmen displayed honesty and integrity in all of their dealings. The customers bought more products from them because they trusted them.

Look for the best in everyone you work with. Give more than you expect to get back and you will never be disappointed. Your foster children may not show you their appreciation today, but they will always remember you. You will have taught them valuable living and surviving skills that they would have not been privy to in their own birth parents' lifestyles.

SUMMARY

Since the beginning of foster care, foster parents have parented from the heart. They have shared their homes and their love with children in need. Most people have felt that love and good parenting skills were the main ingredients for success in this job. Today foster parents need more! They need to understand that fostering children involves much more than parenting your own children does, and that the children are only half of the foster parent's job descriptions.

Foster parent's environments have evolved to be much more complex than just parenting needy or difficult children.

Foster parents must interact as professionals with a child's treatment team. The other professional team members may not view foster parents as professionals. Foster parents daily lives encompass parenting their foster children and working with whole casts of characters who come along with their children's placements.

Many aspects of foster parenting are much different than what most people imagined when they first enter the profession. In order to survive in the foster care system, foster parents must gain a better picture of what the job entails. They must also take steps to get professional recognition from their agencies and other professionals.

We can all agree that there are many factors that make foster parenting a unique and challenging profession. There is certainly a high level of responsibility and accountability bestowed upon foster parents. Individually and as a group, foster parents are not yet fully recognized as professionals. Worse yet, they are often suspect and misunderstood by the general public and by other professionals with whom they work.

We must begin to take the steps necessary to professionalize this vocation in order to preserve future foster care programs and insure that foster parents will be there when the world's children need them. In addition to the desire to provide loving homes for needy children, foster parents must survive the challenge of working and living in the foster care system.

Chapter

2

TEAMWORK

I magine your favorite football team. I am a Arkansan transplanted from Wisconsin, so I will envision the Green Bay Packers. What was it during their glory years with Coach Vince Lombardi that made them such a great team? Talent? Toughness? Love of the Game? Offense? Defense? Great Coaching? They had all of that, but so did many other professional teams!

The thing that the 1960's Green Bay Packers did better than all of their competitors was they played well together! It made them become world champions. Their teamwork set them above all of the other professional football teams. The team shared the dream of winning, and each member set his own sites on that goal. Each individual wanted the team to win, and every one of them performed in a manner that allowed the whole team to accomplish that goal!

Although foster parenting and professional football are worlds apart, there is a common thread. That thread is the necessity for teamwork. The goal of everyone on the foster care team is for a child to come out a winner. It takes a team of professionals working together to make that happen. You, as a foster parent, are sort of like the quarterback. If you don't play well with the rest of the team, everyone loses. Most importantly, the foster child loses.

During the many years I have worked with foster parents and childcare agencies, teamwork has been a critical concept that both foster parents and social workers too often overlooked. Even though it is the very core of how we must operate to achieve our goals of protecting children successfully, we haven't been able to fully attain the ability to perform well as teams.

Foster parents' comments to me in the past have conjured up winning or losing battles over the welfare of their foster children. I have felt this way too as a foster parent. We have to remember that we are fighting a battle, but it is not with our agency, our social worker, or the court. The real battle is to insure safe outcomes for our foster children!

Keep in mind that no one person or entity can do this job alone. Each foster care case requires reporting parties, child abuse investigators, legal professionals, counselors, case workers, birth parents and foster parents, just to name a few. With all of these players involved, it is no wonder that we have to work very hard to all be on the same game plan.

All of the parties involved on a child's case must consider teamwork as the essential ingredient needed in order to insure the best future outcomes for our foster children. Without it, everyone loses. The key to our own longevity in this profession of foster parenting is being able to get along and communicate well with our colleges. If we are not able to do that, frustration with the system will eventually cut short our foster parenting careers.

In our journey to become team players, we will begin by looking at what defines a team. We may all have different ideas of "team." Some people may only relate "team" to sports. That train of thought might lead to winning or losing at something. Others may define "team" as a group assigned to a project connected to their jobs. Ideas about teams may bring to mind competition or getting to the top. Many foster parents I have worked with in the past thought of teams as everyone else connected to the foster care case except for themselves!

The definition of team that I like the best is from a book entitled, *The Wisdom of Teams*, by Jon Katzenbach and Douglas Smith.

Definition: "A team is a small number of people with complementary skills, who are committed to a common purpose, performance goals, and approach for which they hold themselves mutually accountable."

As you may have noticed, there is no coach or winning and losing in this definition!

Let's apply this definition to our foster care team. We are a small group of people. Our core group consists of birth parents, foster parents, social worker or case manager, guardian ad litem, and perhaps a family or child counselor.

This is essentially our ideal foster care treatment team.

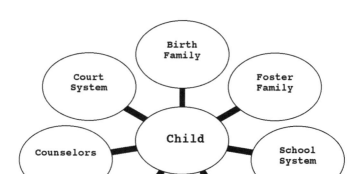

All of the members of our foster care team have individual competencies or skills. Some of us specialize in the daily 24 hour a day care of the children. Others provide case management, legal counseling, teaching, and family training. We each have our own jobs to do. At the same time, we have our own ideas and desires about how the case should proceed.

This group of people is brought together to accomplish a common purpose or goal. In foster care and child protection, foster parents and agencies are both working to protect innocent children and provide them with safe and loving environments until the time may come where their own biological parents can take over again.

THE TEAM GOAL

Members on the foster care team all seem to start out having the same goal. That is wanting what is best for the foster child. But their paths soon divide. While the foster parents are rooting for their foster child, happy in the fact that the child is flourishing in their home, the social worker is making plans for that same child to return home to the birth parents. It is easy to understand how individual members of the team somehow start going down different paths. Unfortunately, those separate paths lead to different goals. Different goals lead to team loss and sometimes even team dissolution.

The foster parent's goal = Keep the child in my home where it is safe and loved.

The social worker's goal = Get those birth parents shaped up so they can have their child back.

The perceived common goal of safety and nurturing for the foster child has become two distinctly separate goals requiring vastly different actions! In order for a foster care team to be successful, each team member must share the same vision of the outcome that they are all working together to achieve!

How do the foster parents and agencies stray so far apart in each of their own visions of the team's ultimate goal? Even though the goal was clearly stated and understood in the beginning by all of the team members, as time passes, they all begin traveling down different paths. Those new paths lead each member to see his or her own picture of an outcome for the foster child.

The foster parents are busy doing the day-to-day chores of parenting. They provide a child with both physical and emotional loving care. They observe the child changing. He is doing much better in their home than he was with his birth parents. The foster parents develop a deep attachment to the child and the belief that their child is better off with them.

Most of the time foster parents, including myself, are very unforgiving of our foster children's birth parents. We see any growth or improvements they have been able to accomplish as never being enough to deserve their children back. We compare them to ourselves and they can never quite measure up to us. In our opinion, their child has a much better chance in life growing up in our family. We view our foster children as worse off with their biological parents.

As foster parents, we slowly begin to claim a child who is not ours to have forever.

Most children love their parents. It doesn't matter how terrible, selfish or brutal their moms or dads have been in the past. They still love their parents and yearn to be with them. As much as the children appear to thrive in foster care, deep in their own hearts, they want to be with their real moms and dads.

My husband, Allen, was in foster care as a child. Over a period of ten years, he lived in fourteen different foster homes. His mother was mentally ill. She managed to keep her life together for up to six months at a time, but then raising her four children by herself would overwhelm her. It resulted in the kids going in and out of foster care at least once every year. (To help you understand more about the bonds between foster children and their biological parents, watch for Allen's new book called, Allen's Story, coming out in late fall of 2006!)

Allen talks about his mom's bizarre behaviors. He said he would wake up in the morning to find her in a trans-like state, chain-smoking cigarettes, sitting in exactly the same spot and wearing the same clothes as the night before. He often felt as though he had to take care of his younger sister, Deanna. Their mom would go into rages for no apparent reason. Allen would find Deanna and get her safely out of their mom's path.

Allen said that no matter how bad it got, he still loved his mom. "She's my mom and I love her. Nothing could ever change that." He said that when he was in foster care, even in the best of the foster homes, all he could think about was how he wanted to go back home by his mother. He was never able to put all of that into words when he was still a child, but his acting-out behaviors said it for him. There was no place like mom and home.

As foster parents, we all lose sight of the fact that children love their parents. They love them no matter what! We are doing a huge disservice to kids by claiming them away from the parents they love. If it is at all possible to reunite a family, that is what we should all be working towards doing. It is the best way to help our foster children with their emotional needs of being able to love their birth parents.

Granted, there are some times when reunification with birth families is not a safe option for children. But even under those circumstances, foster parents absolutely must remain mindful that the bond and love between foster kids and their biological parents is always present. Children are very emotionally fragile where their feelings for mom and dad are concerned. It is an invisible presence that follows them through life.

While the foster parents are focusing on the daily needs of their foster child, the case social worker is busy trying to assist the birth parents in meeting their court-ordered conditions. That is an enormous job! Most birth parents have among their conditions things like finding suitable employment, attending parenting classes, removing persons from their lives who may harm their children, dealing with drug or alcohol problems, and overcoming mental or emotional problems that get in the way of parenting. Many of the birth parents have to learn how to take care of themselves before they can provide safe and adequate care for their kids. The social worker is obliged by the court to encourage mom and dad and to help them remove any obstacles standing in the way of their meeting the judge's conditions to getting their children back. That process consumes the majority of a social worker's time.

Most social workers have to prioritize which fires they are going to put out every day on their jobs. Communication with foster parents usually gets put low on their lists of things to do. You have probably heard the saying, "It's the squeaky wheel that gets the oil." Foster parents don't squeak very much, but plenty of squeaky is going on in the rest of the case.

As a social worker, my daily work with birth parents resulted in knowledge and ideas that didn't all get communicated to foster parents. In the course of my work, I filtered out and told foster parents just what I thought they needed to know. By doing that, many times I left them blind to much of the criteria I used in making my recommendations to the court. At the time it all seemed a matter of time and priorities.

Foster parents usually do an excellent job taking care of foster children without much help from their social workers. Raising families creates priorities for foster parents too. Scheduling appointments, work, and home life don't leave a lot of time for parents in general. When you throw in all of the demands of foster parenting, their time becomes very thinly stretched. Meeting with the social worker is not a priority. It can be put on the back burner unless an emergency arises.

In addition to the time factor, most foster parents know how busy their social workers are. They may view asking for help as being too demanding or they may feel like they are not doing a good job if they have to call and ask questions. For myself, as a foster parent, the least amount of appointments that interrupted our daily schedule, the better.

The result of our different jobs and separate paths they lead us down often causes major misunderstandings between foster parents and social workers. When the social worker calls up and tells the foster parents that their foster child will be returned to his birth parents in two weeks, she cannot understand why they have such a negative response. In her mind she is wondering, "Why are they suddenly, now, having all of these concerns over the birth parents?"

The foster parents have observed their child, week after week, come back to them from visits with birth mom. As a result of these visits they see their child agitated, confused, and naughty. Each visit brought with it having to deal with the aftermath of a damaged child. How could the social worker even consider sending the child back to that situation. The foster parents definitely feel the birth home isn't ready yet.

The social worker is thinking, "Those foster parents are so stubborn. They don't understand the goal of foster care at all!" The foster parents are thinking, "That social worker just doesn't see that this child is better off here with us!"

At that point, everyone on the team feels let down. Tensions have mounted. Potential problems that may have required action were sidelined. Each person on the team has narrowly focused on his or her own piece of the puzzle. The hard work that they were all doing has become fragmented and unorganized.

As a result of not talking to each other and not planning the case together, the team members begin to question each other's motives. They don't seem to be working on the same goal anymore. Each member wonders what the other members are up to. Mutual accountability is lost and replaced by mutual suspicion.

In order to keep the team's goal clear to all of it's members, the team must communicate often and develop trust and mutual accountability among themselves. To achieve the best outcomes for foster children, the team must stay focused on their mutual goal.

TRUST AND MUTUAL ACCOUNTABILITY

The mutually accountable part of our definition of 'team' is where we most often run into problems. To me, mutual accountability requires trust. If I expect to have someone accountable to me and myself accountable to that person in return, I'd better be able to trust that person! Unfortunately when it comes to the foster care team, mutual trust and accountability are not easy to come by.

One or two members of the team are outside the circle of our trust from day one of the case. Foster parents do not often trust the birth parents of their foster child. By their nature of wanting to provide a better life for their foster child, who was abused or neglected, trusting the persons that inflicted the harm is almost beyond reason.

As foster parents, we can easily judge the birth parents and find fault in just about anything they do. Whatever their gains are in parenting ability, they can never measure up to our own standards. "If I am a good foster parent, how can I stand back and allow my foster child to go back to her parent's home that doesn't look anywhere near as good as mine?"

There is a dichotomy in the job of foster parenting. On one hand you have to be a good parent who's main focus is the safety and wellbeing of your child. On the other hand you have to be a good player on a team with people you don't always agree with. It feels like being a good foster parent and going along with the team decisions don't mix well.

The suspicion and mistrust that can develop between foster parents and social workers is a direct result of poor or little communication. It is lack of communication that prompts individuals on the team to be quick to blame, or point the finger at someone else when problems and misunderstandings arise. Foster parents begin to feel as though the social worker is on her own agenda. The social worker feels like all she hears is complaints and criticism coming from the foster parents. Each team member may have legitimate concerns, but individually each person is unable to overcome his or her mistrust that developed as a result of not knowing what the other person knows.

To accomplish the task of working together as a team, the members must be able to establish trust and interdependence with each other. For most people this does not come easily. We are more comfortable doing our own thing and being accountable only to ourselves. We tend to be distrusting and judgmental of each other. How can we become better team members?

Here are some ways to build more trusting relationships with your teammates:

- Always be open and truthful. Speak with kindness, but speak the truth. Hidden agendas don't have any place on the team.

- Spend time with your team members. Invest in getting to know them. Have at least weekly contacts with your social worker, even if it is only a phone call. Attend the team meetings and actively participate in them. Invite your child's guardian ad litem to you home to observe your child. Spend time at counseling appointments for your foster child talking with his or her counselor. Get to know your child's teachers. You will gain a deeper insight to the other members' opinions about the case by talking to them and sharing your own ideas and opinions.

- Share your knowledge first-hand with the person for whom it is intended. Don't communicate through third parties. Facts can sometimes become twisted if not communicated directly. When you have concerns over someone else's ideas, talk directly to that person about it.

- Listen and understand before you speak. Communicate with thoughtfulness and purpose. Don't sugarcoat the facts or use a sledgehammer approach. Understand what the other person is trying to communicate and then add your own ideas or concerns.

- Always, always, always focus on the team's performance. Remember the goal you are all working on. If it becomes unclear, talk about it with your teammates and get it clear. You can all learn to trust each other and work together best by being mindful of your mutual goal and what actions are required individually to accomplish it.

- Respect the ideas and expertise of your co-professionals. Adapt yourself to the team. Don't expect the entire team to instantly adapt to you. Mutual respect between all of you takes time. Consider yourself as professional as the rest of the team.

- Be open-minded and flexible. The other team members may or may not like your ideas. You may or may not like theirs. But, in order to get anything accomplished, you have to be able to consider and respect each other's ideas and expertise.

- If you have a team member who is not communicating, solicit the help of a different team member to get through to that person. If your social worker is not responding to your child's needs or your parenting questions, or if she is tuning out your concerns, you can talk to the guardian ad litem, the social worker's supervisor, administrative reviewers, and other foster parents. Brainstorm for ideas about how to handle the situation. But remember to always go directly to the person you have the problem with first. Then, openly and honestly tell that person that you need to involve a third party. Invite that person to meet with you and the third party.

- See your teammates as collaborators, not as competitors. Look at any group of people and you will see a potential for competition. Students compete for the best grades, siblings compete for their parents attention, co-workers compete for promotions and higher wages. But, team members need to focus more on completing each other rather than competing with each other. In order to succeed for your foster child, you all need to succeed at team membership and achieve your child's treatment goals.

- Above all, listen to each other for understanding, not judgment. Listen, understand, be flexible, and then contribute your own ideas and comments! Most of us are thinking of what we are going to say next while someone else is talking. When we should be listening to what is being communicated, often we are tuning in to our own needs rather than listening for understanding.

Mutual accountability means you must do everything in your power to help your teammates achieve your team's common goal. There is no room for blame or finger pointing. If a teammate fails, the whole team is responsible. You need to be responsible for doing your own job on the team and also for making it possible for your teammates to do their jobs.

One of my children was working on an assignment for school that wasn't going very well. He was partnered with another sixth grade boy on a science project. The teacher called and told me that they were in danger of getting an incomplete grade. When I asked my son why that was happening, his answer was, "My partner isn't getting his part of the project done, so it is not my fault." What he was failing to realize was that if his partner went down for incomplete work, he would go down with him. In his situation, he needed to hold his partner accountable. Did the other boy need help understanding his part? Did he have the tools he required to complete the project? What could my son do to empower his partner? What could be done together to finish the project? He needed to realize that they were mutually accountable for their grade.

Do whatever it takes on your part to help your teammates succeed! If one member of the team fails, you are all in danger of failing. To meet all of a foster child's needs, every member of the team must succeed.

HOW YOU SEE YOURSELF

Maybe you don't consider yourself a part of the foster care team yet. Perhaps no one told you that you belonged on the team. The amount of time that the team requires from you might just appear to be another one of those things that stretch out your limits. Or, you may think the team is everyone else but you. The truth is, like it or not, you can only achieve the best outcome for your foster child and for yourself by becoming an active team member.

You may feel more vulnerable than the rest of your team-mates. The hardest part of playing on this team is that you and your family live in a glass house right on the 50 yard line. The team becomes intimately involved in your life through their associations with your foster child. You and your family are the subjects of close scrutiny by the rest of the team.

You might think that by signing on as a foster parent, you never agreed to this team thing. You just want to take care of a needy child. Let everyone else do the team related chores. I'm sorry to tell you that you won't survive long in this system with that kind of thinking. Maybe what you really want is a babysitting job. The position of foster parenting requires a professional parent who will be able to advocate to the rest of team in the best interest of the foster child. Not everybody is cut out for this work, that's why everybody doesn't do it.

If you want to be a foster parent for the long run, and not to crash and burn from stress, joining the team is the way to survive. You have valuable information that they need for successful planning. If you don't join them as a wholehearted member, they will make the decisions for your child without you. In that case you probably won't be happy with those decisions, but you didn't do anything to influence them. You would only have yourself to blame.

WHO HOLDS THE POWER

"Who holds the power" leads to the question, "How can I have any impact on the case outcome when I don't have any power to make the decisions?" Most foster parents think that the major decisions and the power to make them certainly doesn't fall upon themselves. As much as they would like to have that power, they most often feel that the cold heartless agency has all of the power to make the decisions about their foster children's futures. I would even go so far as to say that most foster parents feel powerless in the decision-making process.

In an ideal situation, decisions for a foster child would be made jointly by the team. After hearing everyone's ideas and concerns, the members would make the choices that lead to attainment of the group's mutual goal. They would form a consensus about what is in the child's best interests.

In reality, the social worker must make some pretty tough decisions. The court rules on custody of the child based on the investigative report filed by the social worker. Conditions for the birth parents to get their children back home are recommended by the social worker and ruled upon by the judge. This process appears to put most of the weight upon the social worker. She also must remove any barriers that stand in the way of the parents success of meeting those conditions.

As foster parents, we tend to give all of our power away. We allow the social worker to carry the brunt of the weight when it comes to decision-making. Then, we complain when it doesn't go the way we want it to.

The persons who hold the power and make the decisions for your foster child don't have all of the information they need to make the best recommendations without your ideas and input. They don't know how your child feels and behaves after a visit with his birthparents. They don't see the child's day to day progress in your home the way you do. They don't experience the child's self-protective defenses and walls. They need all of this information and you are the only one that can provide it to them!

By withholding the things you know and not giving your opinion, you are rendering yourself totally powerless in the decision-making process.

Now I know that you are probably thinking, "I try to tell the social worker how my foster child reacts in certain situations, but she ignores me or minimizes my concerns."

I have heard foster parents make similar statements concerning their social workers enough times to know that the majority of the parents feel like they are up against the wall. I also know that a good many of foster parents do feel powerless in the decision-making process.

The only way to have any kind of influence on the decision-makers is to actively participate on your child's team.

If you choose not to be an active member of the team, decisions for your child will be made completely without regard for your concerns and ideas. The planning for your child will move forward with or without you. Your foster child deserves to have as much information that is available to all team members considered in the planning of his future. Your active participation on the team is critical for the planning and outcome of the case!

As a foster parent, you must view yourself as a contributor and valuable resource to the team. When the team makes a decision based on all of the information gleaned from each of its members, then the power to decide lives within each one of them. The team uses all of its members' ideas and expertise to join their power together and to decide what recommendations to make to the court. Each member possesses power to influence the whole team's decisions!

FOSTER PARENTS MUST BECOME
EQUAL MEMBERS ON THE TEAM

Foster parents must become recognized as equal players by the rest of the members of the child protection team. That is not going to happen overnight. Unfortunately some of the other members may look at foster parents as merely glorified babysitters. During my work as a social worker, my coworkers made two general statements to me about foster parents.

1. Foster parents are saints for what they do!
2. You have to be absolutely crazy to be a foster parent!

Most of us don't see ourselves as saints, nor do we think we are completely crazy, but the black and white thinking that exists among many of he social workers must begin to change.

As a foster parent, you are living with the child who is at the center of everyone's plan! (Remember the diagram of the ideal treatment team.) You know the child better than anyone else on the team. The first logical step to getting the other players to recognize you as a valuable and equal team member is to think of yourself that way!

You are an expert about how that child behaves and copes in your home. You are the only one with that information. The rest of the team needs that information. You need their information as well. In my opinion, that makes all of you equally dependent on each other.

As I discussed in chapter one on professionalism, you have to think of yourself as a professional. You are a professional foster parent. The whole system could not settle for less. Your foster child deserves a professional foster parent. Use the suggestions I outlined in chapter one to transmit to the other players that you are a professional who is equal to them.

If you run into personality conflicts with the other team members, remember that you didn't get to pick your teammates. You do not have to like all of them, but you certainly have to get along well enough to work together. The key is to learn to work with them and trust them while you are doing team-related work. Focus on performance not your chemistry with those persons. Outside of the team setting, it doesn't matter whether or not you like them. Your relationship is based only on matters concerning the team. Set aside your personality dislikes while performing on the team.

You are your foster child's strongest advocate. No one on the child's team, except the birth parents, loves that child the way you do. The stakes are high. The team decisions have a major impact on your foster child's future. Your professional participation on the team is how you can advocate for your child's safety and welfare. If you choose not to participate, your child loses.

With all of these emotionally charged factors, we can most likely agree that team membership is going to be challenging! But I have to tell you that your team participation is critical to the outcome of the case.

FLEXIBILITY

To improve your ability to survive in this job and to get along with your teammates, you must become adaptable and flexible. To quote Michael McGriff, "Blessed are the flexible, for they shall not be bent out of shape." Rigidity and team work do not go well together. Everyone on the team has his or her own ideas based on each member's knowledge of the case and expertise in one's own field. To be heard by the other members of the team, you must first listen to them. Listen with an open mind. If you are intent on meeting with them to get your own way, you will come out the loser. Worse yet, your child will lose.

There are a lot of factors in the foster care case that someone else will know and understand that you may not be familiar with. All of the work done by the team has to follow the letter of the law. Court cases concerning termination of parental rights have been lost or thrown out of court because of simple factors such as not notifying the birth father about a court date, who may not even know he is a father! I observed a case that got delayed over six months because the social worker did not go over the warning of termination of parental rights with the birth parents, even though they fully knew and understood what could happen.

Try to understand what lies beneath some of the decisions that are made. Remember that you are all working on the same goal. At the same time, you are coming together with different view points and different job descriptions. The social service and legal members of the team must operate under strict guidelines. They are protecting children and at the same time working for family preservation whenever it is possible. Your focal point is the child. Their focal points are the birth family, the foster child, you and your family, and the existing laws. Team members listen to each other for understanding, not judgment. Listen, understand, be flexible, and contribute your ideas.

KNOWLEDGE

By human nature, people are intimidated and fearful by things they don't know and fully understand. In your role as foster parent and team member, there is always going to be more you can learn. Knowledge builds confidence and understanding. The more knowledge you acquire and information you have, the better team member you will be.

Knowledge is the key to unlock the doors between you and your teammates.

Educate yourself about what your teammates do. Ask questions and really try to understand their work. Their point of view will become clearer to you when you know more of what they know. You will have a better understanding of your teammates' motives.

At the same time, teach the other team members what you know. Just because a person is an expert in one field doesn't mean he or she understands everything. Remember my example from chapter one of the college professor who changed the oil in his car. He thought the task was absurdly time consuming because he didn't know where to put the oil!

It's like that in foster care. Your social worker or the judge needs to hear your expertise on your child in order to make the best decisions on his or her behalf. Your sharing of knowledge helps them to do their jobs.

Incidentally, if you were to have a better understanding of the Federal and State Children's Codes, you would better understand some of the other components in decisions that are made for your child. The existing laws don't always seem fair. Many people believe that the laws are swayed in favor of birth parents and that children don't have any rights. Although in many ways this line of thought is true, changes have been made over the past few years to make termination of parental rights more fair to children.

One example of that is in the area of birth parents' rights on newborn infants and children under two years old. It used to take over two years to begin termination of parental rights on these very youngest foster children. Babies would turn three or four years old before becoming legally adoptable. Parents were given too much time to get their acts together while at the same time their baby or toddler remained in limbo. Today's laws allow agencies to begin the termination of parental rights after six months in many instances, resulting in babies getting adopted sooner and developing heartier and earlier bonds to their new families.

It is very difficult to support decisions made by the courts that appear senseless. Take steps to learn the court process, understand the laws, and identify with other team members' duties and obligations. It will enable you to know that each person on your team is working to achieve the best outcome for your child within the current structure of the legal system. Then, if you feel angry about how things turn out, your anger will not be at your teammates, but at something that all of you together may be able to change or influence.

Clearly, all of us are not working in a perfect system. I believe that the greatest cause of foster parents leaving the profession is the difficulties they encounter inside of it. Working together with your teammates will enable you to navigate with a little more ease when the going gets tough. If you want to be there for future foster children, you must educate yourself about how the whole system works and work together with your teammates to plan the best possible outcomes for children.

COMMITMENT

In the very nature of why foster parents do this job, lies a deep commitment to help children. The one thing that foster parents all have in common is their desire to give children safe and loving homes. The thing you must realize is that commitment to foster children includes with it commitment to the child's treatment team.

Most of the time our true commitment gets tested in the wake of our trials and adversities. According to John C. Maxwell in The Seventeen Essential Qualities of a Team Player, "People don't really know whether they are committed to something until they face adversity. Struggles strengthen a person's resolve. Adversity fosters commitment, and commitment fosters hard work. The more you work at something, the less likely you are to give up on it." So you, as a foster parent, will need to work very hard on your team membership. According to the famous Green Bay Packer Coach, Vince Lombardi, "The harder you work, the harder it is to surrender." Commit yourself to the team and to the team's common goal of doing what is in the best interest of your foster child. Don't surrender to your team, help them help your child be a winner.

WORKING TOGETHER TO FIND SOLUTIONS

Henry Ford once said, "Don't find fault: find a remedy." When problems arise, why is it that human beings can quickly point at the source of the problem and blame others for their predicaments? A lot of the time we exert the majority of our energy trying to answer the question of WHY things are the way they are instead of figuring out possible solutions.

Problems and challenges can either stop us dead in our tracks, or they can prompt us to think and grow. It's all a matter of how you look at things. On a team, problems can break the team apart, or they can make the team stronger. The beauty of a team is that when one person feels like surrendering to an obstacle, the other team members can come to the rescue.

There is a solution to every problem. According to John Maxwell, "No problem can withstand the assault of sustained thinking." Just imagine what sustained thinking pooled together among the whole foster care team members could produce!

As members of the foster child's treatment team, each and every member must stay focused on solutions. Seeing the problem doesn't take any special talent. The true test is to be able to see options and alternatives for overcoming obstacles.

The best way to stay solution focused is to redefine your thinking. Obviously you can't be in the same state of mind when thinking of solutions to problems as you were when the problems were created. As team players, you all have to get in the solution mode. If you allow problems to stop you in your tracks, your career in foster care will be a short one. If you are truly committed to helping kids, you must become an active team problem solver.

SUMMARY

I hope you have discovered from reading this chapter how important it is for you, as a foster parent, to be an active and contributing member of your child's treatment team. No one can protect our abused and needy children alone. A safe and successful outcome for our foster children is dependent on the work of many professionals, including YOU.

Teamwork is the essential ingredient for successful outcomes in our children's futures. We are brought together as a team to focus on a common goal; That goal is to provide a safe and loving environment for a child in need. All of us on the team must share that common goal and take the necessary actions independently and together to stay focused on our common destination.

We must develop trust and mutual accountability within our teams. Suspicion and mistrust of our team members must be overcome by developing clear communication.

As foster parents, we must learn to know and understand the roles of our team members and the laws that govern all of our actions and efforts.

We must view our teammates as collaborators rather than as competitors. The job of protecting children and providing them with safe environments has no place for blaming and finger pointing. The magnitude of the problems we must face as a team takes all of our collaborative efforts. There is no problem we cannot jointly solve.

We, as foster parents, must see ourselves as equal and valued members of our children's treatment teams. We are not just parents to our foster children, but we are their number one advocates. To truly advocate for them, we must be full-fledged members on their teams!

We must use all of our strength and knowledge to contribute to the decision-making on our children's behalf. It is not enough to just provide for their daily care. We must take equal responsibility in case planning for their futures.

We must remain open-minded and flexible. To be heard by our other team members, we must first listen to them. We must educate ourselves to understand what lies beneath some of the decisions that we all have to make for our foster children. Knowledge is the key that unlocks the doors between ourselves and the rest of our children's treatment team members.

We are clearly not operating in a perfect system. In order to insure our own longevity in this system, we must learn how to survive in it. Working together on a treatment team will make us all more successful in weathering the storms that arise. Our foster children will have better futures through our efforts and successes on our foster children's treatment teams.

We can remain committed and strengthen our resolve to help kids by our mutual work and cooperation on the treatment team. When problems confront us, four or five heads are better than one. It takes each and every one of us on the team to successfully raise our foster children and provide them with safe and loving homes.

Chapter

3

FOSTERING

COUPLE

RELATIONSHIPS

In the course of my career, I had the opportunity to interview hundreds of couples who either wanted to become foster parents or who wanted to adopt children. I know that the decisions that brought those folks to that point in their lives were carefully thought out. All of them had to think about the potential affects on their marriages and families that the addition of neglected and damaged children would certainly bring. The decision to raise other people's children is a major life altering event both for the fostering families and for the children they care for. I believe that couples make the best informed decisions with the information that is available to them at the time. But, like many other endeavors, the reality of the job may be far different and more challenging than what people originally expected. It's like imaging what it is like to fly on an airplane when you have never flown before. I expected that on my first airline trip that I would have the sensation of flying through the clouds at 500 miles per hour.

The reality for me was that it felt like a very big bus that tilts up when you take off and then crawls through the air like a big fat turtle!

Allen and I were in the decision making process for many years before we finally applied for our foster care license. When our biological kids were in grade school at Holy Angles Parish in Darboy Wisconsin, we had already begun discussing adopting another child. At the time we owned a used car business and had eight employees. We had the desire to help kids, but our time was already stretched way too thin. Allen always had the desire to help kids like himself who were stuck in the foster care system. But like many things, having the desire and having the time were two different things altogether.

As our son, Scott, approached adolescence, we sadly recognized that he had some learning difficulties and emotional health problems. At that time there were no labels or conditions that could describe his abnormal behaviors. He had enormous difficulties paying attention in school and with reading and writing. Today his condition is called "Attention Deficit-Hyper Activity Disorder. Back then we had a child with emotional and behavioral problems who required all of the parenting energy the two of us possessed. We felt that our daughter, Kris, often got left in a fog because Allen and I were too busy worrying about Scott's problems.

As Scott and Kris went through their teenage years, Scott's problems with school and his social life only seemed to get worse. While Kris was holding her own, doing well in school and having lots of friends, Scott was barely able to get passing grades. He seemed to link up with other kids who also had emotional problems and were flunking out of school. Allen and I were beside ourselves with worry and constantly questioned what we could have done differently for him. With all of that going on in our lives, our desire to become foster or adoptive parents definitely got put on the back burner!

After long years of struggling through school and society, Scott was finally diagnosed during his early twenties with "Bipolar Disorder" (Sometimes also know as "Manic Depressive Disorder) Even though Scott would be facing a life-long battle with a mental illness, Allen and I got some small amount of relief just understanding that he had a disease which explained his often outrageous behaviors. Getting Scott from infant to adulthood did not leave much time for his sister, much less for foster kids!

I'm sharing our background with you for a couple of reasons. First, having the desire to become foster parents and having the time and resources to do it are two different things. While we were raising our own two kids and dealing with the problems resulting from Scott's illness, there was no way we could take on additional responsibility. Second, we had to consider the affects that stretching ourselves even thinner would have on our two kids and on our marriage. Third, just because the time wasn't right for us then to become foster or adoptive parents didn't mean that it would never happen. Finally and most importantly, I want to demonstrate the fact that the decision to apply for a foster care license didn't come easy. For us there were years of struggle raising our own troubled son, trying to pay enough attention to our daughter, and also running a business that left us emotionally and physically exhausted!

When the point in time arrived that we did actually apply for our foster care license, Scott was 23 years old and Kris was 21. Both of them were married and had lives of their own. We had a huge advantage over most other people considering foster care. We had survived raising our own son who was far more challenging than normal kids, plus I was a child protection social worker with many years experience working with foster families and troubled youth. In addition, Allen had spent over 10 years of his childhood in and out of foster homes. But I want you to understand this: Even with our advantages, we still didn't understand how challenging the job of foster parenting would be! The desire to help kids and all of our experiences were still not enough to totally prepare us for the job of foster parenting!

At the time we applied for our foster care license, we had been married for 24 years and had raised two children. As a married couple, Allen and I were very close. We considered each other " best friend." We were able to communicate with each other comfortably on any subject. We enjoyed the same activities. We liked being in each other's company. We had managed to stay together through our own share of turbulent times. With all of that going for us, we still didn't fully understand the added stress that foster parenting together would place on our relationship as a couple.

With our knowledge of the foster care system and our life experiences, both Allen being a former foster child, and raising our two children, we still couldn't have forecast the challenges we were about to encounter in our new careers as foster parents. I want to emphasize that the actual care of the foster kids was only half of the job!

Again, I want to say that I am not trying to frighten anyone away from foster parenting. If you have the ability and desire to be foster parents, there are plenty of kids out there who need you. I am a recruiter for foster care. I want you to take on the challenge armed with the knowledge you need to succeed and not become another foster care drop-out statistic. After researching foster care programs, foster parenting over 45 children, and actually running a foster care program, I have concluded that the average career life span of foster parenting is between two and five years. In the county where I worked, out of over 100 foster parenting couples, only a handful of the couples had lasted longer than 8 years.

I believe the reasons for foster parents quitting are numerous, but for the purpose of this chapter on fostering couple's relationships, I will focus on how foster parenting as a couple may be far different from what most people expect. I want to try and help you prepare to deal with some of the couple and couple-parenting related issues that are a part of foster parenting.

After couples actually apply for their foster care licenses, most of them can hardly wait to receive their first placement. It is an exciting time. Parents try to imagine what their first foster child will be like. In the orientation to foster care classes that I taught at Fox Valley Community College in Appleton WI, I would assign a homework project to the new awaiting foster parents. I would ask the couples to go home and for the next week, individually, give some thought to what their new foster child would be like. They were instructed to not share their visions or thoughts with their partners. What would each of their new foster children look like? What activities could they imagine themselves doing with the child? How did their child change their lives?

When the couples came back to class the next week, the husbands' and wives' answers to these questions were very different from each other's. Most of the men envisioned a child with whom they were having fun by participating in some kind of sport or activity. The women pictured themselves providing comfort and care to the child. Neither the husbands or wives foresaw a child who acted out or challenged their authority.

Becoming foster parents has some things in common with getting a new puppy. At first you are in love with the idea of owning a new cute and cuddly pet. You envision yourself sitting on your favorite chair petting your fluffy new friend. You think about the fun you will have taking your new puppy for walks or teaching it to play fetch. Then on the first full night of your dog's arrival to your home, you are kept awake all night by whining and yelping. Even though you knew a puppy would be a lot of work, you didn't fully understand how you would feel when your dog would pee all over your new carpet or chew up your couch. You might be soon asking yourself, "Who wanted this dog in our house anyway?" We all tend to forget the negatives and the work aspects connected to owning and training a new pet. At that point you probably come to the realization that you may have underestimated the changes to you family's routine that your new puppy would demand. Owning a new puppy requires a deep commitment from everyone in the family.

Now, imagine the kind of change in your marital routine that a new foster child might require. The boy dad envisioned playing baseball with him probably has many other characteristics and behaviors. Some of them are very undesirable. The child that mom wanted to care for and comfort may have rejected her efforts. The foster children themselves may be different from what you both expected . Also remember from chapters 1 & 2 all of the additional people that will be involved in your lives, looking in at you while you are living in a 'fish bowl.'

The reality of foster parenting is that it has an enormous affect on couple's existing relationships. For those of you readers who are already parents, think for a moment about how the arrival of your own biological babies changed your lives. Adding children to the marriage equation changed the whole scene. The baby's needs became your central focus. The workload increased. New questions and conflicts arose between the two of you over who carried the heavier amount of the childcare chores. Who did more of the 2 AM feedings? Who had to be home from work by the end of daycare? Who gave up golf on Saturdays? As mothers and fathers, you both may have started to keep score over who did more. Along with adjusting to your new routines, seeds of resentment toward each other may have begun to grow.

Not only did your work routines demand change when you became parents, your new child caring routines gave you both more issues to fight and disagree about. Having kids changes the way we fight with each other. Before children came along, either member of a couple could leave the house for a while if things got to be too much. With children present, not only do parents have to watch what they say in front of them, but one of them has to stay home with them. It is referred to by Dr. Ron Taffel in his book, When Parents Disagree, as "Being trapped in the moment." One of you no longer has the option of walking out the door to cool off!

If these kinds of things happen when we have our own biological children, just think about how the addition of a foster child will affect the two of you. A foster child is not your child to keep. He or she comes from a background where adults were not trustworthy. There were no rules or consequences. Routine was something not heard of in your foster child's birth family. Your child did not choose to come into your home. In fact, he would have rather stayed home with his biological parents whom he loved in spite of their past behaviors and with whom he felt familiar. After all, familiar feels comfortable. You and your family are strangers and unfamiliar.

THE DIFFERENCES BETWEEN MEN AND WOMEN

Having more to fight and disagree about with children in our lives calls for a better understanding of our opposite sex partners. You must be thinking that you already know what the differences are between men and women! It seems like knowing that would be the very minimal requirement of becoming foster parents. I'm afraid to inform you that after 36 years of marriage, I'm sure I still don't know all of our differences and don't know if I ever will! Without children factored in, couples still have plenty of issues left to challenge their relationships.

Aside from the most obvious differences between the two sexes, is the completely opposite way in which men and women deal with stress. I think giving you a little information on this topic will help you in all of your family interactions, not to mention the benefits to your foster parenting career.

I'll discuss women first. If you are a woman reader, see if any of this applies to you. When women feel stressed out what do they need? How do they attempt to unwind and unload their worries? If your answer is "to talk about it," you are right on the money. Generally speaking, women like to vent to someone when they are upset or stressed out.

Now consider who a women is most likely to vent her frustrations to. This is how it used to be with me: After a hard and frustrating day working in my county social work office, I would come home and complain to Allen. Some days I started out by saying that I just couldn't do that kind of work anymore. I would tell him about my frustrations with my co-workers and with my clients.

With that in mind, I want you to know that I wasn't looking for advice on how to solve those problems. I just wanted him to have some empathy for me. He would always respond by trying to help. His way of helping was to tell me how to handle the people at work, or telling me not to worry so much about it. That is the same way that most men typically would react. Men are problem solvers. When women come to them to vent, men respond by telling them what to do about whatever they are talking about.

What I really needed from Allen back then was not him coming up with solutions to my problems at work. I needed him to say something like: "It sounds as if you had a really hard day," or "You poor baby, how can I make you feel better?" I needed him to understand how I felt.

When his response was unsolicited advice, I would become more upset and frustrated and so would he. He was trying to help, but it wasn't working for me. Men, listen up. When women are upset or frustrated, they need you to listen to them. They want to vent out all of their pent up worry and frustrations. All you have to do is indicate that you understand. Listen to your partner without offering advice, unless she asks you for it.

Otherwise her venting and your advice will leave you both feeling defeated and frustrated. The mere fact of you being there and listening is what she needs!

Men, now it is your turn. What do you need when you come home after a difficult day? What do you want from your wife? According to John Grey, in his book, *Men Are From Mars; Women Are From Venus*, when you have a problem to resolve, you want to go into your caves where you can forget about what's bugging you for awhile. Dr. Grey says that men cope with stress by temporarily trying to get away from their problems. They tend to become more agitated while mulling things over in their minds. Usually they do not want to talk about whatever is on their minds. Men try to get temporary relief from their problems by escaping them through an activity such as watching a ball game or messing around out in the garage.

Here is how it used to go at our house when Allen was upset about something. He would be unusually quiet. When I knew something was bugging him, I would talk to him and try and pry out of him what he was thinking about. I would follow him around the house trying to make him talk, but instead of talking he would eventually walk out of the house to get away from me. He would go find something to do in the garage. Instead of leaving him alone to temporarily escape his problem, I drove him out of the house by grilling him.

Men do not like to ask for advice. They want to be left alone to solve their own problems. Did you ever notice that when the two of you get lost while driving, it is usually the wife who has to ask someone for directions? Men don't even like to admit when they are lost, much less ask a stranger for help. So women, don't stalk after your men to try and pry out what is bothering them. Let them go to their caves and do whatever they do there.

When women talk about their problems, men respond by feeling blamed for the problems. Men feel compelled to help solve the problems when their wives really want someone just to hear and understand them. When men hibernate and do not talk about their problems, women feel as though their husbands are shutting them out. What men really want is to be left alone for a while and have time to work out their own problems. Because of their differences in coping with stress and how they respond to the perceived needs of each other, husbands and wives can easily fall into poor communication patterns. It takes conscientious work by each partner to give the other partner what he or she needs.

Now I will apply how these differences in coping styles come into play when the kids become involved. Check out this scenario:

Mom comes home at the end of the day after work and finds the kitchen a disaster area. Crumbs are all over the floor, dirty dishes are stacked up in the sink, and her teenagers are laying around in the living room snacking on potato chips and watching MTV. She can't even find a clean spot on the kitchen counters to set her bag of groceries down. She immediately starts yelling at the kids and complaining to her husband. "No one ever cleans anything up around here except me! Can't I get a little help around here?" Dad turns on his heels, not wanting to deal with any of it after his own hard day at work, and heads out to the garage to start changing the oil in his car. Mom responded by yelling and venting. Dad responded by exiting. Each is doing what men or women typically do when they are stressed out. (By the way, this is an example from my own house.)

By hearing his wife vent and yell, dad probably felt that she was blaming him for the problem. By her husband walking out the door, the wife felt she was unworthy of love. It all goes back to our gender differences of dealing with problems and stress differently.

Mom and Dad both got caught up in a situation where they each individually needed something different. Dad wanted peace and quiet. Mom didn't want to walk into a messy house where everyone was laying around snacking. Sometimes our different needs and our insensitivity to our spouse's needs can get us into arguments that could be avoidable.

In our example, Mom could have directly told the kids to get up and help her. Dad could have supported her by telling them that they need to help more around the house. He could have told her that he understood that she was frustrated about the mess and that he was thinking about a problem at work and walked right past it without noticing the mess. He would have appreciated her not going off in a verbal tirade the minute she hit the door.

Both parents in that situation got caught up in each of his or her own needs without regard for the partner. It is very easy to respond in that manner. Most of us do it automatically every day. We inadvertently create more tension, and in the aftermath, stand there wondering what went wrong. How did everything get out of control so fast?

THE DIFFERENCE IN HOW MEN AND WOMEN PARENT

Along with our gender differences in coping styles, there are also gender differences in how we parent. When it comes to dealing with the kids, women generally take a more immediate problem-solving approach while men generally take a more character-shaping approach. Our different approaches have a lot to do with the amount of time each parent has to spend with the kids.

Here is how it might go with mom: While she is in the kitchen at six o'clock pm trying to thaw out pork chops in the microwave, while throwing together a salad and setting the table for supper, her two children are fighting over who gets to play with the legos. She is in the middle of what I like to call 'multi-tasking.' She hears them fighting, dries her hands and goes to the playroom. She separates the two of them and divides the legos between them, telling them that if she has to come in there again to settle their squabbles, she will take away the legos and put them both in a time-out. She has an immediate solution that is no hassle. The problem temporarily goes away, which is what she needs at the moment. She can now go back into the kitchen and finish preparing supper.

Dad might handle the same situation more like this. He is watching the evening news between channel surfing with the remote control. When the two children start fighting over the legos, he goes in the playroom and gets both of their attention. He gives them a short lecture on the importance of sharing. He is trying to instill in them that as they get older, they need to learn to give and take. He wants the solution to the fighting to be a lesson in sharing. He encourages the kids to share the legos and play nice together while he keeps a close eye on them to make sure they go in that direction. His parenting solution takes more time, but at that particular moment, he has the time.

In these two examples, neither parent is wrong. Their differences are actually complimentary to each other. The children need both 'stop bad behavior' actions and 'life lessons'. The difficulties arise between spouses when parents disagree in front of the children, criticize or attempt to overpower the other.

Kids absolutely must see both parents as having the power and ability to take care of them. If mom or dad criticize the other in front of the kids, it's as if one parent is stripping power away from the other parent. When you disagree about child-rearing issues, never ever do it in front of the kids!

If mom dominates over dad's actions and decisions, the children will learn that they can do it too. The same thing goes for dad overruling mom. The surest way for the kids to lose respect for parents is for the parents, themselves, to rip away the other partner's power.

Men and women have their different parenting styles and in addition, they may each think differently about how to parent. One may believe in corporal punishment while the other has a no hands on approach. Each parent's basic philosophy about how to raise children properly can be drastically different, or slightly different. Even when a couple started out thinking they shared the same values and ideas about child rearing, in actual practice and daily living, it is possible that a couple's philosophies may begin to drift apart.

In addition to styles and philosophies about how to parent, there will be times when one parent is more emotionally involved in an issue with a child than the other parent. A situation may require action from the parent with most invested in the problem. In her book, *Grounded for Life*, Louise Felton Tracy, M.S. talks about 'one parent ownership of a problem.' The problem is more important to one parent than to the other. She used an example of dad's tools having been left all over the yard by his son. It pushed dad's buttons far worse than mom's. Some problems are better off to be divided ahead of time. Dad deals with tool use and care, Mom deals with whatever is immediately important to her. (For me it is a clean kitchen.) Decide which parent owns the responsibility and care of the problem. That is the parent who deals with it.

Because Allen gets more frustrated over lost or broken tools, he is in charge of all tool-related problems with the kids. I let him know when I see his tools laying around outside rusting, and he takes it up with the boys. On the other hand, I get real upset with the boys when they neglect our animals. I am in charge of our cats, horses, chickens, and ducks. When Allen notices our animals were not fed and watered properly, he tells me and I deal with whichever boy slipped up on his job.

Parenting sounds so easy in principle. But, once you think you finally have things under control, new challenges with the kids arise and it seems like you are starting all over again. As a couple, your temperaments are different, your reaction times are longer or shorter, your tolerance levels are higher or lower and your emotional needs are almost the opposite of each other. With children in the picture there is more to disagree about. No wonder parenting is so difficult at times!

One final thought before we move on to parenting foster kids: I have yet to meet the perfect parents. Don't feel as though you have to be anywhere near perfect to become foster parents. If you have observed parents that appear too good to be true, then they are probably too good to be true! If you have the desire to help kids, the willingness to learn, the stamina to hang in, and enough humbleness to admit when you are wrong, you may be just what the foster care agencies are looking for.

THE ADDITION OF FOSTER CHILDREN
TO YOUR MARRIAGE

Did you ever hear a social worker say, "Treat your foster children just as if they were your own?" If you were licensed by my former agency you could probably say yes to that question. I had foster parents in the county program that were told they had to take their foster kids along on their annual family vacations. Before I was a foster parent myself, I didn't see anything wrong with that. Now I have seen the error in my ways! Ask any foster parent if they need a vacation from their foster kids and I know the answer will be a resounding "You bet your boots I do!"

There are areas that call for the same treatment between your biological kids and your foster kids. They all need your love and attention. They all need nutrition and exercise. But there are some huge differences:

1. Your foster kids have another set of real parents who they still love in spite of how unfairly they were treated. Most of the kids will have at least weekly visits with their parents. 95% of foster kids will go back home to their birth families and there is a great likelihood that you will lose contact with them and not be provided with information about how they are doing in the future. (This is beginning to change in some areas of the country. Judges and social workers are beginning to realize that any positive adult influence on a foster child's life should not be severed.)

2. Your foster kids come into your home with lots of emotional baggage that you didn't have anything to do with creating. Most of them will carry their baggage with them well into their adult lives.

3. Your foster kids have behaviors that you probably never dealt with in your own family.

4. There is an army of people guiding you and watching you as you parent your foster child. You will have restrictions about discipline with the foster kids. You may be asked to discipline them in ways different from how you discipline your own biological kids.

5. The trust level you established in your home prior to foster care most likely will not be able to be extended to all of your foster kids. (Don't feel too bad about that, they won't trust you right away either.)

Because foster parenting is not just like parenting your own kids, each of you must carefully evaluate the impact that foster children will make on your marriage and family. Make sure you and your spouse both know how the other feels about taking on the challenges of foster children. Talk about your own expectations and understand your partner's expectations. How do each of you view your own role and what do each of you expect from the other?

Many perspective foster parents and even those who have lots of experience often fail to realize that this profession can challenge even the most stable marriages. If you have unresolved problems in your marriage, work them out before you even consider getting your foster care license. Adding foster children to the mix will only compound those issues.

Among the hundreds of foster parents I recruited and guided, I have witnessed several divorces. It is fair to say that those couples were probably headed for divorce anyway, but foster parenting certainly poured gas on their fires. If you are having difficulty communicating with each other, foster care will add more complicated issues that require an even higher level of communication between the two of you.

Foster parenting together is different and harder than parenting your own children. It's like climbing a steep mountain without any safety ropes. Even in the best of circumstances, parenting a foster child will raise some new issues in your marriage. Before you begin on this journey through foster care, above all else, you'll both need a strong commitment to each other. In addition to that, you both need to be in total agreement about your intentions to become foster parents in the first place. It won't work if only one of you has the complete desire and commitment. You must become each other's safety net.

Foster children will come into your home with a huge amount of emotional baggage. They have learned to mistrust all of the adults in their lives and that will include both of you. Some of them subconsciously hate or mistrust either men or women in general. For example, if a child's father has deserted him, he may transfer the anger he feels toward his biological father to all men or to a particular substitute father figure. Thereby, he may be more compliant with his foster mom and more hateful toward his foster dad.

It is possible for each parent looking at the same child to see a different child! A foster daughter may get along horribly with her foster mother, but be perfectly angelic and compliant with her foster father.

Here is an example: After driving her foster mother crazy all day with bizarre behaviors and refusal to comply to foster mom's requests, five year old Becky gets the consequence from Mom of an early bedtime for her bad behaviors. As soon as her foster father gets home, Becky jumps on his lap and with big brown sad eyes says, "I love you daddy, do I really have to go to bed early? Mommy grounded me and I don't even know why?" Little does he know that mom was tortured all day by this same sweet little girl's nasty behaviors. He responds to her saying, "I'll talk to mom and see if I can get her to let you stay up later."

I'm sure you can see where this is going! Each parent has responded to the same, but different child. I have observed this kind of scene replayed a hundred fold in my own home. Unsuspecting parents end up interfering with each other by the way each one of them views a particular situation.

Dad says to his wife, "Honey, don't you think you are being a little hard on Becky? She is only five years old!" Mom angrily responds, "You don't know what I've been through all day with her. Don't be telling me I'm too hard on her! You are too easy on her!"

Perhaps you have had a similar conversation in your house. Same kid, different behaviors, different responses, resulting in each parent responding to his or her own experiences and getting off on different channels from each other.

In addition to appearing differently to each parent, foster children have huge issues that lay beneath the surface of their behaviors. Regardless of how your foster child appears to each of you, or what diagnosis he or she carries, there is a lot going on in a foster child's head that the two of you are not able to see or understand. Your foster child will not be able to put his or her fears, needs, or emotions into words. What is buried deep in your foster child's psyche will come out in the form of behaviors.

My husband, Allen, told me the story of how at the age of eight, he was placed in a foster home with a nice family. His younger sister, Deanna, was placed with a different family. When a few weeks had passed and they were not able to see each other, Allen went down to a factory warehouse in Milwaukee and threw rocks in to the majority of the plate glass windows on it. He was angry because he couldn't see Deanna. He wasn't sure who he was angry at, or how to resolve his problem, so he got it all out of his system the only way he could. His anger came out by destroying hundreds of dollars worth of plate glass. His foster parents at the time had no idea what was going on inside his head. Allen may have not understood his feelings and behaviors himself. All he knew was he wanted to see Deanna and he was very angry.

Remember that this chapter is not about solving children's bizarre behaviors, but about how parents need to work together as a team when reacting to their foster children's actions. Think about how each one of you would feel and react as you read the following excerpts that actually happened in our home:

While dusting shelves in our six year-old foster son's bedroom, I pickup up a sports cup. You know the kind. You get them free with soft drink promotions. It had a plastic cover and a straw sticking out of it. It felt heavy as I lifted it from the book shelf, like it had a clump of clay in it. I opened it up to find a clump alright, but it wasn't clay, it was feces! When I asked our foster son about it, he said that it wasn't his cup and he didn't know how it got there. The same child from time to time would pull his pants down, hang off the side of his bunk-bed and poop on the floor.

***

We had a problem in our house with candy, soda and snacks disappearing from our refrigerator and pantry. While I was changing the sheets on our two teenage boys' beds, under one of the mattresses on the bunk-bed were literally 40-50 Little Debbie snack wrappers, and empty juice containers. When I asked the occupant of that bed how all of that got there he told me his brother must have done it. I asked his brother how the stuff got there and he said, "I don't know anything about it."

***

It seemed like anytime I took a hard look around the boy's bedroom, I found things that were not normal. One time I saw that the little door on the VCR player looked half open when it usually looks closed. I reached my hand inside to discover my sister-in-law's missing cell phone. Neither one of my boys knew how it got there. To make matters worse, both of them had spent that very afternoon at her house helping her search for it!

***

One day my sixteen year old boy, who was planning to go on a field trip at school the next day, announced to me that the principal told him he couldn't go. I asked him why. He told me that there was this girl who was thirteen, who keeps trying to get him in trouble. She allegedly tells other kids and teachers that he is doing stuff like touching her inappropriately. This girl doesn't even go to his school, but she rides the same school bus. He says he doesn't go near her because he doesn't want her to make up stuff about him. I asked him why she would do that, and he said that he had no idea why.

***

One of our adopted daughters ran away one night. We found out later that she had gone to her girlfriend's house and located her birth mother on the internet. She wrote her mother and told her we were mean and abusive to her. Her birth mother called child protection services and reported this. The next day, instead of her getting questioned by the social worker on why she ran away, we were the center of attention. What were we doing that caused her to run away and tell her birth mother all of that stuff? Instead of bringing her home to our house, the social worker insisted on me meeting her at the police station. After we talked and she felt comfortable about my daughter coming back home with me, she handed my daughter her business card and told her to call anytime she felt threatened.

***

Now, this book is supposed to be about everything but the foster kids, but I used the previous examples to help you understand how foster children's behaviors can affect your marriage and family. Imagine how you or your spouse would have reacted to any of these situations. Could it be that you each might have had your own method in mind of how to handle the situations? Can you imagine how much more stress could occur between the two of you than did in your pre-foster child days?

Another factor that will affect your marital relationship is that fact that as foster parents you are living in a fish bowl. You may have heard this term before. Everyone on the outside of your family is watching nearly everything you do. When you argue with foster children present, the issues do not necessarily stay within your own walls. Kids hear things and repeat them without discretion. Events in your own home can become more than your own family's business. To make matters worse, some foster children like to get the dirt on you. They get a feeling of power by making you look wrong or maybe their birth parents don't seem so bad if they see you get into trouble too. Foster parents' lives are put under a lot of scrutiny. Can your marriage hold up under those circumstances? (Read Chapter 5.)

In addition to these questions, you and your partner have different tolerance levels. Some days one of you may feel like throwing in the towel and quitting foster care while at the same time the other partner wants to keep trudging forward. For Allen and I our different tolerance levels actually enabled us to stay foster parents longer. On days I felt like quitting, he would bolster up my emotional strength and I did the same for him. Fortunately we usually both didn't get down in spirits at the same time!

Another issue that can get between husband and wives is the ability our foster kids have of pitting one parent against the other. The "mom said/dad said thing! Communication between spouses under these kind of circumstances is critical. The importance of parenting together on the same channel is essential to the success of foster parenting.

PARENTING ON THE SAME CHANNEL

For those of you who have decided that this job of foster parenting will work for you, and for those of you who decide not, but have children in your lives, I am going to share with you some ideas from one of my previous works called "Parenting on the Same Channel." If you are interested in obtaining this complete training article on-line, go to fosterparents. com and click on "Parenting On the Same Channel.

To begin parenting on the same channel, the most important thing to understand about solving any problem is that the problem itself is not the worst part. We tend to make our real problems bigger by turning to our old solutions that haven't worked for us in the past. Anger and frustration result, making the original problem with the kids bigger than itself. The best way I know of to not fall back into our old patterns that haven't work for us in the past is to "Be Prepared." (That is the old Girl Scout coming out of me.)

Do some preplanning for the possible challenges your children will throw out at you. If you are thinking that you don't know what those challenges might be, just look at some of the stuff you have dealt with in the past. Namely, undesired behaviors that don't go away easily. What kind of behaviors come up again and again that are difficult for you as a parent to deal with?

Avoid getting into crisis situations with your kids without a plan for your how you will act. Without a prepared plan, parents often 'react' to their children's behaviors. The kids push parent's buttons and the parents go into automatic anger or frustration modes. It is very hard to keep a cool head and make good decisions while you are in the middle of a turbulent situation. Having a plan on hand allows you to switch into your problem solving mode rather than your buttons pushed mode. Here is an example of a plan we worked out:

We have a plan we worked out together, ready for use when our kids lie to us or blame each other for things. Our oldest two boys lie about everything. They lie about homework being done, about who broke something, about who said what, and even that the color red is green! During these lying events, everyone in the house becomes prone to losing their tempers.

My husband is very good at handling these situations. He came up the plan I am about to share with you. We decided that when a situation comes up and we do not know which kid to believe, we follow this course:

Jake and Jared will be seated in separate rooms, so they will not be able to compare notes or hear each other's story. They will sit on kitchen chairs so they are not overly comfortable. This prevents curling up and falling asleep when bored. They will be able to get up when both of their stories match. Every 20 minutes they each receive an opportunity to tell one of us what happened. If their stories do not match, they have to sit there another 20 minutes. This plan works exceptionally well when they have plans to do something later in the day, or if their favorite TV show is about to come on. If the truth doesn't come out, they do not go anywhere or do anything.

Now if this plan sounds harsh and unfair to the one who told the truth, maybe so. The thing to keep in mind here is that they both have had a long history of telling lies. They have both put the other in this position many times in the past. This plan has prevented a lot of screaming and hollering in our house. It also gets to the truth, and saves the one who is telling the truth from the same fate as the liar. The liar gets some amount of reprieve for finally coming out with the truth.

Planning ahead for your foster children's behaviors allows you to 'act' rather than 'react' in response to them. Design your plan for handling bad behaviors with your children by coming up with it together. Make sure you both agree on the plan and understand how each of you will implement it. Here is another example of one of Allen's and my plans:

Our oldest adopted son, Jake, often gets on Allen's nerves when he is helping work in Allen's shop. We have a plan in place that when Allen starts becoming frustrated at Jake's lethargic work attitude and when Jake becomes mouthy and rebellious, Allen simply turns him over to me for different chores. I keep a list of yard and household chores ready for just that possibility. My list consists of lawn moving, changing the cat litter box, scrubbing the bathroom and other unpleasant yard and household chores. Hopefully after getting turned over to me enough times, Jake will realize that working with his dad in the shop is more pleasant that scooping out cat doo-doo.

We have another plan for when I get to my boiling point with the kids. If Allen is present when he sees me about to loose control with one of the boys, he gives me a chance for an escape. He will say something like "I know you have work to do in your office, why don't you let me take over here for a while." Because he isn't the owner of the problem that was going on at the time, (usually a mess in the bathroom or kitchen) he has the ability to maintain a cool head which enables me to escape to my office while he and the boys get the mess cleaned up.

There are plenty of other times when one of us is home alone with the kids or when we are both about to blow which requires another type of plan. It is called a 'Parent's Time-Out.'

Time-out might bring to mind punishment, but 'Parent's Time-out' is no such thing! It is more of a mini-vacation away from the war zone. It is intended for one or both parents to escape the scene, cool off, and think calmly about how to deal with the children's negative behaviors.

Here is how it goes: Eleven year-old Jamie comes home from school with a note that he instigated a fight on the playground with another boy in his class. This is the second time in the same week that he has gotten himself in trouble at school. I am still upset from the last incident, and I want to scream at him. I decide instead to take a parent time-out. I say to Jamie, "Jamie, I am so angry at you right now, I'm afraid of what I might do, so I am going in my room for awhile to think about all of this. I will come back out in a little while and we will talk. Then, I will decide your consequence." I do not say another word to him and quietly go to my room.

This plan of action has a two-fold benefit. First, it removes me from a situation where I feel like grounding him for life. I get the luxury of time to sort out what I will do. Second, Jamie is baffled because I didn't start yelling at him. Surprised by my calm reaction, he gets to worry about his consequence while I am quietly in my room planning his fate. He is sweating it out while I am calmly thinking, maybe even taking a bubble bath to boot!

The following are the steps to complete a parent time-out:

1. Have a place in mind before you actually need it where you can go and shut out everyone else.

2. Recognize when you are about to loose your temper with your child and call a time-out for yourself.

3. Exit the scene from your child calmly, leaving him or her to worry about what you will come up with for a consequence. (I like to leave my kids sweating it out while I am in my time-out.)

4. Above all, don't get sucked into an argument with your child. Simply say, "I am going to take a quiet time-out, and I will get back to you later about this problem."

5. During your time-out, use up some of your angry energy by taking a walk or calming yourself in whatever way works for you. Use the time to coherently come up with a plan for solving the problem with your child.

6. After your time-out is over, go back and calmly talk to your child. Sometimes just asking your child what he thinks should happen will solve the problem for you.

Time-out work great between husbands and wives too. The plan works a little different from time-outs with the kids. When a couple begins to reach a boiling point during an argument with each other, either partner can call for a time-out for any reason. Once the time-out is called, there is no further discussion. No one talks or gets off a parting shot.

You should pre-plan your time-outs together. Here are a few things to try:

• Set up in advance how long each time-out will last. Do this before you need to use one.

• When the allotted time is over, you will both come back to an agreed upon location free from children where you can talk.

- Neither of you may use the phone or complain to anyone else during the time-out. Venting or complaining to a friend or neighbor only serves to fuel your fires. It may also add more ammunition to fight back and prove you are right which won't help the situation at all.

- Do something physical during your time-out. Work such as cleaning the kitchen or garage physically allows some of your stress to escape. Taking a walk or another form of physical exercise would also be good. When I am working off my frustration my house gets real clean.

- At the end of your time-out, begin talking to your partner by pointing out one small aspect of the problem that you both agree on.

- Agree to disagree about some things. Try to both wholeheartedly support whatever plan you negotiate.

- Make sure you both understand the plan and know what is expected of yourself.

- Present a united front to your kids.

Another way to begin parenting on the same channel is to remember that you are parents, but you are also still a couple. You got married because you love each other. While you were dating, you paid attention to each other. You listened to each other. You tried to put your best foot forward regarding each other. You were a couple before you were parents. You are still a couple. You have to work at that relationship even harder than you work at parenting. Spend couple time together without the kids. After our thirtieth year of marriage and parenting more than forty foster children over the years, Allen and I started dating each other again. Once a month, one of us would plan a special date. It would be a secret until the day of the plan. For one of Allen's dates, he planned a convertible ride to Mattoon Wisconsin. That was special for me because I have a picture of my ancestors moving a house on logs down a dirt road there. For one of the dates I planned, I took him bow hunting, which is something we both love. The dates don't have to be fancy or expensive. They are merely a nice thing to do for each other that features spending time together. Try dating again. (Each other of course!) While you are out on your dates, listen to each other. Look at each other. Give each other your undivided attention. Act just like you did when you first dating.

Becoming retuned-in to each other will make you both stronger parents. When it comes to parenting foster children, you will need that strength as a couple. When problems arise in numbers with your foster children, prioritize. You can't fix everything at once. To make things easier on both of you, decide together which of your foster child's behaviors need to change first. What does your child need to change for everyone to be safe? What behaviors grind on either one of you the most. Pick out one or two immediate behaviors that you want to extinguish and both of you work on that until the behaviors go away. Then move on to the next behavior you want to start or stop. Bite off small pieces that you both agree to work on. Kids have very short memories coupled with deeply engrained habits and behaviors. Understand that you cannot change everything at once and most importantly stay focused together working toward the same goals.

When one of you is interacting in a situation with the children, the other should not butt in or try to help unless invited to. You both want to appear capable of handling problems. Remember earlier when I explained the differences between men and women. What does each of you need? Men need to feel capable. They do not appreciate unsolicited advice or criticism. Women need to feel loved and appreciated. If you women readers want to feel love and appreciated, do not butt in! If you men readers want to feel capable and respected, do not offer unsolicited advice. The bottom line here is: Neither of you want unsolicited advice and neither one of you should try to give it!

You need to build each other's confidence in the ability to parent, both in your own eyes and in the children's eyes. Your partner may not welcome your interference. If you disagree about how your partner is handling something with the kids, talk to each other later in private about it. There have been many times at our supper table with the kids that my husband and I silently disagreed as to where the other one was heading with a problem. We used the silent "evil eye." It was a signal for, "drop it for now, and we'll get back to you later." If we discussed our different opinions in front of the kids, they would have had an excellent opportunity to fuel the fire.. Remember, kids will capitalize on your differences. They love to use the divide and conquer technique!

During an extreme crisis, give yourselves the gift of time. In my own experience, problems that seem gigantic in the initial moment usually shrink in size after a little time goes by. What appears insurmountable at three o'clock might feel more doable at 4 o'clock. I also find that sleeping on a big problem shrinks it down. The subconscious mind is very powerful. One time I was trying to think of a man's name all day. It bothered me until I went to sleep that night. At two o'clock in the morning, I sat straight up in bed from a sound sleep, and said, "Jim." That was the person's name! My brain was at work while I was resting. Now that I know how well I think in my sleep, I let some of my difficult decisions go overnight. Some things just seem to work out better the next day.

When it comes to discipline and consequences for kid's bad behaviors, consistency between the two of you is a must. Your kids need to understand: "If I do X, then Y will happen." It doesn't matter who imposes or enforces 'Y', just that 'Y' is consistent between the two of you. Neither of you want to be viewed as either too soft or too strict by your kids. You both need the respect from your kids to enforce the house rules and impose the same consequences. In *Love Busters*, by Willard F. Harley, he says, "Decisions about discipline are often made independently, without a joint agreement....When that happens, the spouse doing the protecting often feels the pain of the discipline more acutely than the children do. And the other one doing the disciplining feels totally unsupported." This is a sure way to build a wall between the two of you, while at the same time losing your status of competent parent with your kids. Your foster children especially, need consistent routines and discipline. You cannot let them see disagreement or power struggles between the two of you. Rules and consequences will most likely be a new concept for them. They need both of you to agree and enforce the rules consistently.

Learn to let go of some things. With foster children there are lots of issues to deal with. Some problems don't need instant solutions. Some of them we can learn to live with. Others may go away requiring no action on the part of parents. Our energy as parents gets drained so fast that we must learn to apply it where it will really counts.

Some of us are bigger control freaks than others. This is particularly something that hits home for me. I am one of those control freaks! However, over time I have learned that being in control all of the time over everything is impossible.

It is not fun for me and those around me when I become over-controlling. It is easier to distract myself from some of the things I want to control than to stress out over them. Richard Carlson, Ph.D., in his book, *Don't Sweat the Small Stuff*, says this, "Life is filled with opportunities to choose between making a big deal out of something, or simply letting it go, realizing it doesn't matter." If you choose your battles wisely, you'll be far more effective in winning those that are truly important to you. You will become a more affective parent and better loved by all.

It is especially important to let go of some of the child related issues. I know that I drive Allen nuts when I lose it over crumbs on the floor or the boys wearing pants with holes in the knees. In the overall scheme of things, some stuff is just not important! No one else cares if my floor is swept clean. It doesn't matter if the kids look like refugees as long as they are playing at home. The board of health will not condemn our kitchen and the kids will eventually turn out to be spiffy dressers on their own. Letting go of some of the unimportant things will make your parenting partnership much more enjoyable. When one or both of you become caught up in the small stuff, the tension gets to be too much!

Parenting, especially when it comes to foster children, can be challenging for the best of us. Surviving as a couple, even without factoring in our children, has only a 50/50 chance at success. With all of our differences in thinking and coping, men and women have to work at just plain getting along with each other! When adding in our own children and/or foster children our couple relationships become even more threatened. Foster parenting requires strong parenting skills and strong relationship skills. Parenting on the same channel is an absolute must!

While working at our couple skills and parenting skills, we must continue to learn and adapt to change. Those of us who thrive will have committed time and energy to nurturing ourselves and our partners. In order to do that, each one of us needs to accept our own shortcomings and those of our significant other. We will learn to give each other gentle guidance and strength. Working on our couple relationships will make for better parenting teams. Couples will be able to combine the best of what each partner has to offer the kids and better actions during times of crisis. By parenting together on the same channel, both of you and your children will all come out winners.

I have reflected on mine and Allen's own years of marriage and parenting together. There have been times that required compromise with each other, faith in our future, and just plain hard work on our couple and parenting skills. I firmly believe that Allen and I could not have been successful foster and adoptive parents without diligent work on our connection to each other!

A final word on this subject: Allen and I did not arrive at the point of having better couple and parenting skills overnight. If you see yourself needing improvement in these two areas, you can make a commitment to reach a higher level of communication with your partner and your kids at whatever level you are starting from. I know there is lots more we can all learn to become more affective parents. There was an old saying that things get better with age and time. I think along with age and time we must make constant efforts to learn and grow. Do what you can to grow in knowledge and be patient!

Chapter

4

FAMILY, FRIENDS, & EVERYONE ELSE!

As we have discovered, foster parenting affects us in ways we may have not thought about prior to committing to the job. There will be reactions from our biological children at home, our grown up children, our brothers, sisters, parents, friends and neighbors as well. This chapter will be about some of my own experiences with family, friends and others and also about those similar relationships that foster families have shared with me. I will help you take a close look at how others may react and treat you when you are a foster parent. I will give you ideas about how to help the important people in your life accept your vocation as a foster parent and how to deal with friends and family members who either decide to keep their distance from you or shut you out of their lives altogether.

As I related in earlier chapters, I have experienced difficulties with my co-workers, friends, immediate family and extended family as a result of Allen of and I becoming foster parents. We had new relationships with social workers, teachers, law enforcement officers, and many others who were not previously involved in our lives. All of the changes and challenges to our existing relationships can be overwhelming. This chapter will demonstrate to new foster parents some of the relationship challenges those who have gone before you have faced and how they dealt with the important persons in their lives. For you readers who are already seasoned foster parents, I predict that you will identify with many of the forthcoming stories.

IMMEDIATE AND EXTENDED FAMILY

I'll start by sharing a story about our biological daughter, Kris. She was 24 years old and married with a young daughter of her own when we adopted our daughter, Brenna. During the time that Brenna was our foster daughter, Kris and her got along fine. After Brenna's adoption, Kris seemed a little more distant to her and slightly angry with us. Finally one day Allen asked Kris what was bugging her. Her reply was, "Dad, I thought I'd always be your only daughter." Even though we had discussed the adoption with the entire family, and everyone agreed that Brenna's becoming a permanent member of our family was what we should do, Kris still had some negative feelings she did not discuss with us then.

The relationship between Brenna and Kris finally began to blossom when Kris was able to talk to us about how she really felt. It gave us the opportunity to tell her that no one could ever replace her in our hearts. Brenna helped the situation too. She was twelve years old at the time and was the type of child everyone loved. She admired Kris, who worked in law enforcement, and wanted to be just like her when she grew up. Kris soon referred to her as, "My sister, Brenna."

Our granddaughter, Bre, grew up with foster children. Her parents, Kris and Bill, were foster parents to a 18 month old girl when Bre was also 18 months old. The two young girls were almost like real sisters, except that one of them had to go away for visits on Sundays with her birth mother. Bre became conditioned to her foster sister going to visit her 'real' family. One day when Kris had the two girls in the grocery store, Bre got frustrated with her mother because Kris wouldn't buy her a treat. Bre angrily cried out, "If you don't buy me a treat, I'll go back to my real family." Even though she was with her real family and didn't know anyone else, she imagined that she had a different real family who would give her what she wanted. It struck us all as funny at the time, but the words Bre said demonstrated very well that young children are affected by foster siblings in ways we don't fully comprehend. She must have thought that she was a foster kid too or that everyone, including herself, had another 'real' family.

Our son, Scott, was 26 years old when we adopted our first child. His only response was to ask us why we wanted to take on troubled children and have all that stress in our lives. He provided us with enough challenges himself, and he must have thought that he completely wore us out. He seemed less affected than his sister, Kris, but to this day I am not one hundred percent sure about that.

The most accepting members of our immediate family were Allen's father and step-mother. Allen had been in and out of foster care from the ages of 6 to 15. His father disappeared from the scene when his parents divorced. Allen's mother did everything in her power to discourage her ex-husband from visiting their four children, even to the extent of deliberately sabotaging any attempts he made to do so. After many years of foster care, Allen was reunited with his father, Henry, at the age of 15. His stepmother, Mae, legally adopted Allen and his younger sister, Deanna.

It was amazing to me that Allen's family, troubled by their own past nightmares, were the most open to welcome our adopted children into the family. They became our greatest supporters by providing respite care for us when we needed to get away. They were actually involved in raising our adopted family. The kids thought of them as Grandma and Grandpa.

On one Easter Sunday, when Henry was in the hospital, we traveled 75 miles with our adopted sons Jake, Jared and Jamie to see him. When we arrived, he was still alert but only less than an hour from his death. When the boys walked into his hospital room, Grandpa's eyes lit up and he smiled. He recognized the boys and was happy to see them. That is the way I want to remember Henry. He loved our boys.

My father grew to love our adopted kids too, but his story is very different from Henry and Mae's. We lived about one city block from my father and stepmother. My dad was widowed by my mother's death and he remarried about five years later. He and his second wife, Millie, (not her real name) were not warm and welcoming to our new family. Millie was the type of person that constantly criticized everyone for everything. She ruled over my father who was not an outspoken man. Even though we attempted for years to build a relationship with her, our efforts only caused us more frustration. She took out her anger at us on my father.

We felt as though my dad was unhappy and stuck with Millie. She would actually un-invite us when it came to the holidays while she would be busy entertaining her own family. On my father's 72nd birthday, he was served with divorce papers from Millie. He was raised Catholic and did not believe in divorce. My dad became a devastated and lonely man.

I think he would have preferred being with her and remaining an unhappy married couple had she not taken the step to separate.

The good thing that came out of my father's divorce was that he became accessible to all of his own kids again. We did not have to run the interference with Millie to see Dad. I soon had a standing Thursday night dinner invitation at his house. I taught Foster Parenting Classes at the local technical college on those evenings. Between my regular social work job and teaching, Dad would make me supper. We did that for two years. I remember it affectionately and was glad to have Dad in my life again.

We soon included my dad in family dinners, trips to our cabin, birthdays, and everything else with our foster and adopted kids. They began to call him Grandpa too. He accompanied us to their school concerts and other events they were involved in. During those last two years of his life, I think the kids helped fill his lonely hours. Our two adopted daughters went to his house every week and cleaned for him. He took them to the local Dunkin Doughnuts for a treat. Our boys took turns spending Saturday overnights at his house which they thoroughly enjoyed. Grandpa watched the Three Stooges and old western movies with them. He played his harmonica for them too. When my father died, our adopted kids felt the loss of a grandparent who loved them.

My father's funeral, as many funerals do, provided for a family reunion. My brother, Joe, and his wife, Paula, came from Florida with their two year-old son Luke. Luke was born when both of his parents were in their forties. He was a miracle baby who came to full-term after Paula had two previous miscarriages. Joe was thrilled to have his first child.

Dad's funeral was the first time we were all together since we had adopted our second family.

Joe and Paula were very intrigued with our 'motley crew' adopted family. They asked many questions about how they could go about adopting another baby. I explained to them that healthy American babies were difficult to adopt, especially if a couple was in their forties. I told them to consider foster care or special needs adoption as an alternative. They went home thinking about the possibilities.

A few months later, Joe and Paula became foster parents. They had several very young individual children and two sibling groups come and go from their home. Then six week-old Cyrus came along. He was placed with them by Broward County as a medical risk. They did not expect him to live more than one month. Joe and Paula took turns staying with him during his frequent emergency hospitalizations.

Today, Joe and Paula are the proud adoptive parents of three year-old Cyrus. Luke has a new forever brother. Cyrus has grown into a healthy and rambunctious toddler who loves his Uncle Allen and Aunt Mary and all of his adopted cousins, especially Jake. We were all there in Ft. Lauderdale last year for his adoption celebration. I'd like to think that we were a strong influence on Joe and Paula's decision to become foster parents and go on to adopt their son. We have all grown closer as a family and now make a point of getting together one or two times a year instead of one or two times a decade! In addition, we talk on the phone nearly every day sharing our parenting experiences and giving each other encouragement when each of us in turn needs it.

I have another brother, Jim, who is a 5th grade teacher. Jim is single and childless. He is a greater than average teacher who is well respected in his profession. He became Brenna's godfather and he had a good relationship with the rest of our kids. Some teachers and others professionals as well, don't understand the parenting challenges that foster and adopted kids present. I am grateful that Jim got to see first hand some of the family crises we faced. Although I don't think he always understood our motivations and parenting techniques, he was always involved as an uncle to our kids and remains supportive to Brenna who is now married and raising her own child.

Our family took another curious turn that I would like to share with you. After we had adopted 17 year-old John, 12 year-old Brenna, 11 year-old Jane, 7 year-old Jake and 6 year-old Jared, we had one of our regular family meetings. Seventeen year-old foster daughter, Melissa, and her infant son were also part of our family at that time. The kids got together and decided that for the time being we should not be foster parents anymore, except for keeping Melissa and her son.. They realized that the foster kids took a lot of our time and attention, and they felt that they needed all of it. They didn't like the disruptions that foster kids brought into our house. They wanted things to stay just as they were on that day.

It's funny because at that time we were really burning ourselves out and couldn't see it. We had a problem saying "no" to the agencies who wanted to place kids with us. Most of the kids who came to our home had no where else to go except group homes. We felt we had to give them all a chance. Our kids opened our eyes. They made us see that they needed our undivided attention. They had more than their share of emotional, social and academic challenges. We needed to give them 100% of our parenting efforts. We took a family vote and the unanimous decision was to quit foster care after Melissa and her baby left. We all felt a strange sense of peace and relief. So you see that even our adopted kids were affected by our foster parenting.

I have to mention that it did stay that way for a while. But after John was on his own and Brenna and Jane were teenagers, we went on to adopt 8 year-old Cheyenne and 6 year-old Jamie. I believe that is the end of the line for us. Jake, Jared and Jamie remain in our home today. We are looking forward to raising them to adulthood and reclaiming our empty nest again!

CO-WORKERS

We survived all of the family reactions and relationships, but one challenge in my own life was getting through to my co-workers. If you remember from the previous chapters, during the time Allen and I became foster parents I was working as a social worker in child protection at a county agency. I later became the foster care coordinator for the same county's program. Some of my co-workers were very supportive and interested in our foster kids. Others were down right insulting.

I had a few social workers say right to my face that "You must be crazy to want to be a foster parent." These were the same social workers that had their client children placed in foster homes in our county. They were the same workers who were supposed to value our foster homes and support them in their needs. The same few people at work, when referring to some of the foster parents in our program, would make comments such as, "They must be doing it for the money." At times I felt like an alien at my own workplace!

It was a double edged sword because I was the recruiter and trainer for the foster parents. Both the foster parents and the social workers came to me with their problems. Knowing how some of my co-workers really felt about the foster parents made it very difficult for me to prepare the foster parents to deal with the social workers' negative attitudes. None of those social workers had ever had a foster child. Some of them were not yet parents or even married. Most of them had been supported by their parents through their college years, and they had no idea how other people might have had to struggle with issues such as getting an education, finding employment sufficient to support a family, or having alcohol or abuse issues under their own roofs.

I heard a senator on Fox News this morning talking about how Hurricane Katrina may open our eyes to how poor people live. He compared this tragedy to John Steinbeck's novel, *The Grapes of Wrath*. In summery he said something to the affect that just as the novel opened our eyes to the rural desperately poor, Hurricane Katrina opened our eyes to the poor and disenfranchised citizens in our urban populations. Here was this wealthy senator who was elected by a majority of not wealthy folks saying we don't know about poor people! I couldn't understand how he could make a statement like that when his job is to serve all people. If he doesn't understand the predicaments of our most needy citizens, what is he doing in a job where he is supposed to represent all of us? I feel that the same goes for social workers. If a person cannot understand why people take in foster kids, or is not able to realize the difficulties and challenges that foster parents face, then that person has no place in the profession of foster care social worker.

I truly felt that more than a few of my co-workers thought of foster parents as a disposable commodity and/or as a nuisance. They expected our foster parents to solve most of their own issues with the foster kids, and complained when they had to help them find solutions. They did not understand what all of us foster parents know above everything else. That is, we do foster care to help kids. We parent from our hearts. In the process, we expose ourselves and our families to the scrutiny of educators, social work agencies and others because we want to help neglected and abused kids.

With that much said, I also want to stress that there were as many or more of genuine and caring social workers than the cynical ones. It was obvious to me that my co-workers who put care and effort into their relationships with our foster parents and did their best to support our foster homes were recognized and valued by the foster parents.

Struggling with the issues between my professional work world and my foster parenting world eventually lead me to a new career. I have dedicated myself full-time now to educating foster parents. I am committed to teaching them the skills they need to survive working with agencies like my old one, while at the same time parenting difficult foster children who require of them an additional new set of skills! I am working to build value and professionalism in to the job of foster parenting.

As a foster parent, you may find yourself undervalued or thought of as crazy by your co-workers too. I found that sharing things about my home life and foster children was not something I could do straight across the board with all of my co-workers. I learned not to get into conversations about foster care issues from my home life with the cynical people at work. Too much information to those people only made my job more difficult.

Keep in mind there are confidentiality issues involved when you discuss your foster children's backgrounds with others. When I talked about my foster kids in this book, I changed their first names and never used their last names. When you find yourself open to receptive ears and non-judgmental caring co-workers, make sure you keep the conversation about your foster child very general and do not ever reveal confidential information about the child's case.

Your co-workers may be inquisitive about your foster care world and they may appear to be interested, but remember they are not all coming from the same place you are. Some of them are genuinely interested and will hold you in high esteem for what you are doing to help kids, but others might just be nosey and superficial. You have to sort out people's motives who appear interested in hearing about your foster kids. Once you are able to accomplish that, you can become very selective about with whom you discuss your personal home life issues.

Just as I stated earlier, foster care is not your entire life. The same goes for your job. You have a life outside of your place of employment. If your two worlds of work and foster parenting do not mix together well, don't try to put them in the blender at the same time! When you have a need to talk about home and foster kids, find a person who will listen with an empathetic ear. Most certainly, not all of your co-workers will qualify for that role!

OLD AND NEW FRIENDS

Having said that, my attention will next turn to friends. When I think back to all of the friends I have had during my lifetime, not all of those people stayed actively involved with me through my entire life's journey. Some friendships have endured all twists and turns in my life while others have quietly faded away. As I continue to meet people and make new friends, I maintain a cherished memory of my friends from the past with whom I have lost contact, but for whom I still hold a place in my heart.

In particular I think about the people I knew and loved during my college years. I was in my thirties then, and my interests and needs were very different from what they are now. My circle of closest friends then included a Spanish-study friend, a geology instructor, a younger Chinese immigrant, a single mother, and a man and his wife whom I had met in our mutual classes. Back then, between this group of friends and my family, I didn't have much time for anything except working as hard as I could to graduate. That was my whole world then.

I have lost contact with that entire group of friends. We all stayed in touch for a little while after graduation, but as time went on our contacts became fewer and further apart. We all moved to different parts of the country and went on to have very different careers. I lost the need for frequent contact with my study-partners and began to meet new people in my new after-college world.

The point is that friendships are not static. Sometimes they grow, sometimes they change, and sometimes they fade into our memories. Our current and past friends are all important to us, but some of them don't fit well in our present life styles or present states-of-mind. As we all grow and change, so do the circles in which we travel.

When Allen and I became foster parents, naturally our interests and focuses changed. Our empty nest quickly bulged at the seams. Our existing social life changed too. The circle of friends we had then did not have huge households of dependent children like ours. They were able to be spontaneous when it came to going out for dinner or weekend trips, where we had to plan well in advance. Even our friends who had children only had one or two of them. They didn't have teenagers who ran away from home, smoked pot, or had criminal records. If they did have teenagers at all, they didn't want to expose them to our troubled kids.

Our invitations to dinner and social events quickly dwindled down to zero. Some of our friends thought we had totally lost our minds or that we had taken steps backwards in time having to become parents again. We understood where they were coming from. Foster parenting isn't for everyone. At the same time we still had the desire for some kind of social life.

Soon we found ourselves in the center of a new social circle. Through our associations with other people like ourselves, we began making many new friends who were also foster parents. It was no big deal to get together with a family who had four or five kids when you had four or five kids too. Most of our get-togethers became more like large family reunions with kids running around all over the place and huge pot-luck suppers being consumed.

All of us understood that our foster children, as a group, had huge social and emotional problems to overcome, while each one of our kids had his or her own individual personal challenges as well. All of us wanted to help these kids who lead us to be bonded together as friends in a common mission. Not only did we become friends, but we also became each other's pseudo extended families!

Along with our new found friendships, we received the added benefits of our new foster parent friends' trials and errors with their foster kids. For many of our problems, we didn't have to reinvent the wheel to find solutions. We also acquired empathetic listeners who understood the challenges we faced in our home. In return, we shared with them our successes, failures, advice, worries, and hopes!

After years of friendship and foster parenting, many of us have moved on to other friends and challenges. But I'm sure that the bonds we were privileged to form with our foster parent friends and families will be among those relationships that endure through the years to come. If any of my long lost foster parent friends are reading this, I highly value your friendships and the lessons you have taught me. Thank you!

NEIGHBORS

As neighborhoods vary in socio-economics, races, beliefs, and other make-ups, so will your individual neighbor's reactions to having troubled children into their close proximities. Originally upon becoming foster parents in Appleton Wisconsin, we had wonderful neighbors. Next door on one side was a parking lot to a grocery store and on the other side was a newly-wed couple who were friendly and at the same time minded their own business. We had a golf course across the street that ran the whole length of our block. No one from there seemed to know or care about our foster kids as long as we all kept off the grass.

Things went well for us with our neighbors while we lived in the city. It wasn't until we planned our move, along with our 5 foster and adopted children, out into the country that some small problems erupted. We had an accepted offer to purchase a large home on five acres. But, when the owners got another offer later that same day from a physician and his wife, who had no children, they tried to renege on our contract.

The property surrounding that five acres was owned by family members of the seller. We felt that they were trying to discriminate against us because we had so many children. Luckily, our realtor went to bat for us. She made them understand that there was a signed contract that they could not break. She also pointed out the possible discrimination charges we could raise if they didn't sell to us. We ended up with the home and property, but we also got some disgruntled neighbors to boot. It resulted in them keeping to themselves and us living on an isolated parcel of land right in the middle of them.

We remained there for seven years and really never knew any of them. They were quick to report to local authorities whenever one of our kids stepped a foot onto their properties or crossed a yellow line on the road. We managed living next to them by keeping our distance and not over-reacting to their complaints. We had to keep careful track of our kids making sure they stayed in our own territory!

Although our own experience was unpleasant at times with our neighbors, we never had any major problems. That wasn't the case with some of the foster parents I worked with in the county program. There was one family in particular that I remember about whom I received daily complaints from their next-door neighbor. The incidents that were reported never had any substance to them. It seemed as though the complainer was trying to drive the foster family out of the neighborhood.

There was another foster family that we knew for years, and with whom we were very good friends. They took excellent care of delinquent teenaged boys. Their neighbor lady found out somehow that one of the foster boys had been accused of molesting another teenager. The boy was below average mentally and was never allowed to go out on his own. The neighbor lady did not have any children living in her home, but she had horses. She complained that this boy was a threat to her animals and to herself just by his presence next door. She was a constant thorn in the side of the foster family and caused them stress over a situation that was not nearly as threatening as her own neurotic imagination. Even so, these two neighbors live side by side today and she and her horses have never come close to being violated. As time passed, our friends learned to go about their own business and ignore her hollow complaints.

I also used to get complaints from various neighbors of foster homes over the parenting techniques some of the foster parents used on their foster kids. Some neighbors thought the foster parents were too strict while others thought the foster parents were to lenient. The neighbors, who didn't actually live 24 hours a day in the same houses with these tough kids, sometimes thought they knew better ways to handle them. I had to find a delicate and diplomatic way to tell them to walk in those foster parent's shoes before they judged them. As Allen and I had done ourselves, I talked to the foster parents about not over-reacting to their neighbors and keeping close eyes on their foster kids so as not to pour fuel on their fires.

Whether people are foster parents or parenting their own biological children, there will always be others who don't agree with their parenting styles. Because of this fact I have told foster parents not to take it too hard when people openly criticize them or disagree with them over the parenting techniques they use. As long as they are not breaking any laws or committing any unethical acts, their neighbors should not cause them undo concern. I think life becomes difficult when foster parents think too much about what their neighbors think of them. If we are going to truly commit to helping kids, then we have to take the necessary steps to do so regardless of what our neighbors think of us in the process. We are accountable to our agencies' policies, the law, and our own moral standards. Let the neighbors think what they want. As foster parents we must carry on with our missions of helping kids.

TEACHERS AND SCHOOL PERSONNEL

Much unlike our neighbors, as foster parents, we cannot ignore our children's teachers or go about our businesses without caring over what they think of us. The relationships between foster children, teachers and foster parents call for some amount of agreement and common ground. Hopefully we are all working on the same goals for our foster children. As inhabitants of the 'fish bowls' or 'glass houses' that I previously discussed, our lives become more public and open than the lives of other everyday citizens. Our children's teachers, living on the outside of the fish bowls, sometimes look at foster homes and foster kids with a higher amount of scrutiny than they look at other non-foster family's kids.

As foster parents, we have to be prepared to handle this more public life and higher scrutiny that our status's demand. Most teachers desire the same thing we desire when it comes to our foster children's academic lives. That is to have our foster kids perform at their highest potentials and abilities in school. Usually by responding to teachers' concerns and by open communication we all get along fine. But there will certainly be some occasions of discord or misunderstandings.

In addition to living in a fish bowl, our foster children get more noticed at school for another reason. The majority of them have emotional and behavioral problems. They don't blend in well with the rest of the kids. By their very natures, they call more attention to themselves. Most of my foster and adopted kids were well known to the school counselors, principals, vice principals, and even the police liaison officers.

When we had four teenaged foster sons living with us, it wouldn't have been unusual to get several calls a week from someone in authority at their schools. The problems ranged from poor academic performances, being AWOL from classes, not eating lunch, eating two lunches, to throwing chairs at teachers. One of us, that being Allen, had a full-time job communicating with school personnel, thinking up appropriate consequences, enforcing those consequences, and living with one or more angry boys who were constantly grounded.

On the last day of school in June 2005, our 11 year old adopted son got a free16 mile ride home compliments of his elementary school principal. Jamie had brought a paper bomb to school that morning. When the cafeteria supervisor noticed it under his chair, she called the police. It said the word 'bomb' on it, had wires coming out of it, and had a 9 volt battery inside of it. When the police officer interrogated Jamie, he said that he brought the fake paper bomb to school because he wanted to finish coloring it and taping it. He further explained that we didn't have any tape at home. Furthermore, he had to finish the bomb that day because his cousin was coming from Florida to visit and he needed the fake bomb to be able to play war with him.

That whole bomb incident got Jamie a lot of attention. We had to have a conference with his school counselor and the elementary school principal the next day. Because Jamie was a 5th grader and moving on to the middle school in August, we had to have a conference with the principal of that school too. Shortly after school started, we were asked to come in to meet with the middle school counselor about providing special services for Jamie. At that meeting, we were informed by the school counselor that the meeting was called because of some of the comments Jamie's fifth grade teacher had forwarded to the middle school. Based on those comments, the counselor was thinking that Jamie might need extra psychological help.

Jamie's math teacher and the vice-principal were also in the meeting with us. His math teacher had a copy of the freshly printed mid-term report card that had just come out. We all noted that Jamie was on the honor-roll. Everyone in the meeting stated that Jamie was doing great this year. We all agreed that he doesn't need any special services. Personally, I think he has more tolerant and understanding teachers this year. For a boy like Jamie, teachers who can let him know they are in charge and keep his energy focused do not have much trouble with him. The point is, the whole meeting was called based on the notes from last year's teacher, who had never asked for a meeting. There is a huge difference among teachers. Where his school personnel last year were thinking they might have the next Eric Rudolph or Richard Reid on their hands, his teachers and vice-principal this year are willing to let him show them that he can be successful.

It is a 100% probability that foster parents will need to become involved with their child's school, and I don't mean volunteering in the cafeteria! Foster kids are more visible and they have issues. As a foster parent, you will be in close contact with school personnel.

Furthermore, you might get a reputation that precedes school officials actually meeting you in person. That fake bomb incident demonstrates that very well. We hadn't met our elementary school principal in person prior to Jamie's bombing incident. When I went to have the conference with her, I explained that Jamie was adopted. I told her that he came to our home at the age of six and had been removed from six other foster homes because of behavior problems. I went on to tell her that I am a former child protection social worker and have extensive experience working with troubled children. I wanted her to understand how far Jamie has come from his past behaviors. I told her what we are doing at home with him regarding his behaviors and also in helping him to deal with his past losses.

When I was ready to leave, she stood up to shake my hand and said, "Thanks for coming in. I have a whole different picture of Jamie's home life than what I had imagined." Until we met in person, she grouped our family into the 'troubled family-messed up parents' category. She had based her opinion about Allen and me on Jamie's bomb scare and information she had previously received from Jamie's teacher.

As a foster or adoptive parents, you absolutely must get acquainted with your child's school personnel. Not only will that help you stay on top of potential problems with your sons and daughters, but it will demonstrate to the teachers and other people there that you have your child's best interests in mind. Don't allow them to put you into that 'troubled family-messed up parents' group by default! Let them get to know you.

Here's another reason for the school to know you better. Sometimes foster kids will try and get sympathy at school, making you look like a villain. For instance, one of my boys was eating a second breakfast when he got to school and running up a charge tab. When the school office called and informed me that we owed $25.50 for breakfasts for Jake, I asked that person why they allowed him to charge that much without our permission. She replied that if he wasn't getting breakfast at home and he was hungry, they would allow him to eat there and charge it. I told her that we always made sure the boys had a big breakfast at home. She said, "Well maybe that isn't enough." I instructed her to not allow Jake to charge breakfast. I told her that it is my job to make sure he gets breakfast before he leaves the house and that he will not go hungry. I had to assert myself because she was already of the opinion that we were not feeding him enough!

Before I leave the topic of school and teachers, there are two short stories I want to share:

When Jake was in first grade, the very first semester of school he had after coming to live with us, he was giving his teacher an awful time. Whenever she asked him to do something he didn't want to do, he would collapse on the floor and throw a major tantrum. After trying to deal with him for the first few days of school and not getting anywhere with the problem, she called Allen. He told her to call him immediately the next time Jake acted in that manner. She did just that. When Allen got the call he went directly to the elementary school. Jake was in the hallway, on the floor, still refusing to comply with his teacher's requests.

Allen said to Jake, "What makes you think you can act like this?" Jake said, "I don't know." Allen firmly looked him in the eye and said, "I am not going to allow you to pull this stunt again. The next time you try something like this, your teacher is going to call me right away. When I get here, I will stay here all day to make sure you listen to her and behave yourself! Now if you can get your act together and do what you are told, for this time I will go back home and see if you can handle it yourself." That was the last time Jake ever threw a tantrum at school. If he even became close to losing it, his teacher would threaten to call his dad, and Jake would immediately straighten up. I guess the thought of having his dad follow him around all day cured the behavior.

As equally important to curing Jake's behavior was the fact that Allen had promised to come directly over to school when

Jake's teacher faced that problem. She understood that we would do whatever was possible on our parts to help her control Jake in the classroom. If we hadn't responded and allowed a first grader to terrorize his teacher, we would have been put in that TFMUP group (troubled family-messed up parents).

This second story is similar, but it demonstrates how this method of getting kids to shape up in school works well with teenagers too! There was a foster mother who was a stay-at-home mom to four teenaged foster sons. She took in some of the most delinquent teens in our program. When her boys got into trouble for not showing up at school, she would threaten the boys with something that insured they made it to class. She told them that if they didn't start walking directly to school and staying there, she would personally walk them to school with her hair in curlers, wearing her striped bathrobe and pink bunny slippers. I can still picture her in my mind. She obviously didn't care what her neighbors thought!

The threat of embarrassing kids for their own good can go a long way. Those four boys started showing up at school. Of course, they got into other trouble, but that clever foster mother had a wealth of methods for handling their challenging behaviors. I'll save those for another book! In the meantime, just remember to keep in close touch with your foster children's schools and that it doesn't take rocket science to come up with solutions. (If you join a foster parent support group, you can learn from foster parents, like the pink bunny slipper lady, who have gone before you and solved some of the same problems you will face.)

There is one final area that I must discuss about schools. Some school districts are more heavily burdened with troubled kids than others. Some teachers are more receptive to new foster kids coming and going throughout the school year.

Because of the wide variety of situations and people you will run into, don't put a negative label on all of them if you encounter one or two bad experiences.

For example, when I was the foster care coordinator for a large county in Wisconsin, I ran into a problem with one of the county's smaller city school districts. It seems that particular school district thought they had too many foster parents living in their city. One day I received a call at work from the principal of the high school. He flat out told me not to license anymore foster homes in his district. He said that there was a disproportionate number of foster kids in his school, and he intended to not accept anymore!

Recruiting foster homes is very challenging to say the least! Not everyone is willing or able to take in troubled kids, especially teenagers. I did have several foster homes in that city, who took delinquent teenagers, and in addition, the Oneida Indian Tribe was partially in that county and some of their foster children attended that city's schools too. I could not allow that principal to think he could get away with banning future foster kids from his city!

First of all, my point is that his bad attitude and refusal to take more foster kids was the first I encountered during 13 years working in that county among nearly fifty different schools! I had to reinforce to myself that there were many more good souls out there who did a great job educating our foster children. Second, I wasn't going to let this self-righteous pompous man get away with what he was threatening.

I immediately scheduled a meeting with him. I prepared for that meeting by reviewing the statistics about foster children in other schools, speaking to our county's legal advisors, and planning for an appeal to any ounce of humanity that the principal might have possessed.

Our face-to-face meeting went much better than our phone call. I personally think it is harder to be rude and cold to someone who is sitting right in front of you! I explained to him that other schools were indeed enrolling foster kids without fussing and that they too had their fair share of the burden (as he called it.) I told him that even if he did have a disproportionate number of foster kids, that the numbers were never static. Foster kids come and go. There may be times when one school has more kids, but in another semester they may have less. I explained that we, as a community, were very fortunate that his city had kind-hearted and generous people who were willing to take care of delinquent teenagers in there homes, and the least that he could do was provide an education for those children. I told him that I was sure the mayor of that city would be proud of our foster parents too. In the end, although not happy about it, he backed off the topic and faded into wherever retired principals go.

So you see, that foster parents are not always valued by everyone. I put that principal in the MUSO (Messed Up School Official) category. I want you to know that he was by far in the minority of the rest of the educators in my county, the majority of whom wanted to teach kids no matter where they came from. Sometimes, as foster parents and advocates for children, we must stick together and assert ourselves!

PUBLIC OPINION AND THE MEDIA

A lot of attention becomes drawn to our foster kids by their teachers. After all, school is where they spend more than half of their waking hours. But usually the school problems get resolved between foster parents and school personnel without much other public interest. I want to stress again that 99.9% of foster parents are doing wonderful work with their kids. But, did you ever notice that the .01% who mess up, seem to affect the general public's opinion about all of us? There doesn't seem to be a week that goes by that the television and print media have one or more stories about bad foster homes.

It's kind of like bad Catholic priests. Out of the massive number of priests in the world, a handful of them abuse kids, and the rest of them also become subjects of public suspicion. Now days, parents could be more proud of their children being car salespersons rather than members of the clergy! (Not meant to offend car salespersons; I have been one in the past myself.)

In my old county there was a story about a foster father who was discovered sexually abusing teenaged boys. In addition to his foster sons, he had abused some boys at the high school where he was a police liaison officer. This all happed several years after I had left my job as foster care coordinator, but I'm sure I would still be taking the heat over it if I was still employed at that county. There are bad cops, there are bad foster parents, and there are bad people. But, we can't label the whole barrel of apples bad if we find a worm in one of them. We never hear much about the apples that aren't rotten! We should not hold this one man's deeds against foster fathers or police!

This week in the news, along with Hurricane Katrina, there were two stories that caught my attention. The first one was about a couple who owned a nursing home that allegedly allowed 45 elderly residents to drown in the flooding of New Orleans. Can we generalize that information to all nursing home staff? Would all of them run away to save themselves and leave their patients alone to die in their beds? Of course not!

The second story was about an adoptive home who had 11 children from the ages of 1 to 14. It was discovered that some of those children were sleeping in cages at night. The parent's defense immediately was that their psychologist told them to do that because the kids were autistic. In my mind not only are those foster parents whacked out, but so is any agency who placed 11 autistic children with one family in the first place. That couple will have their day in court, and there may be several placement agencies involved. But in the meantime, foster and adoptive parents once again are getting slammed by the media.

Over the past weekend a well known host on a Fox News show made a statement about that case which reflects how some people think about foster and adoptive parents. To paraphrase his comments, he said that many of these adoptive parents get financial subsidies from State and Federal governments. He further stated that some of these adoptive parents could rack up an annual income of $80,000 or more by warehousing special needs children.

Although I am a Fox News fan, I want to stop the 'spin' on how much foster and adoptive parents are reimbursed for taking care of the most difficult children. Think about how far $80,000 a year goes now days. Just for a moment consider how caretakers of special needs children spend their $80,000. A foster couple with just two or three special needs children have their hands full 24 hours a day. They would not be able to both work outside the home. In addition, they would need to hire outside qualified help every time they stepped out of their house together. You can't have your next door teenage neighbor baby-sit. Babysitters or caretakers for foster children have to undergo training and background checks in most states. Usually they will not work with special needs children for anywhere close to minimum wage. If you added up minimum wage for one person 24 hours a day, seven days a week for a year it would equal over $61,000.00. I want to emphasize that one person couldn't handle the children alone on a full-time basis. Now add in normal expenses like mortgage, food, utilities, insurance and mini-van payments and you will understand that full-time care of special needs children is not a lucrative endeavor for foster and adoptive parents!

There are greedy and uncaring people in this world who will use any means to try and get rich, even if it involves mistreating others. But, hear this loud and clear: Nearly all foster parents who I have encountered are doing their jobs because they want to help kids! The money they receive doesn't even come close to reimbursing them for all of the costs associated with caring for their children. Many foster and adoptive parents are taking in children who have been shuffled around in the system because of their special needs and challenging behaviors. The majority of special needs adoptive and foster homes have children and adolescents who are getting their last chances at living outside of institutions that cost much more tax payer money than warm and caring foster parents.

Remember from my survey of foster parents, the number one reason people become foster parents is to help children in need. I also asked the foster parents on that same survey how highly they rate their reimbursement from the county or state. All of them agreed that what they were paid barely met the extra expenses they incurred having foster kids. Most of them felt that if they were just looking to make money, there were much easier ways to do it!

I appeal to the media to not judge all foster and adoptive parents by a few extraordinary examples. Tell the stories, but balance them with stories about the good that others are doing when it comes to offering love and homes to very challenging children. Don't poison your audience with generalizations and uninformed opinions.

Sensationalism in news stories is what makes us watch, read and listen. It doesn't sound sensational to have a news story about a family who is working hard with two biological children and a foster child unless something dramatically out of the ordinary happens to them. Unfortunately if something bad happens, that is what we all remember because we will most certainly hear about on the news.

While I was in college, I worked at a residential treatment center in Sacramento California. There was a counselor from the same firm who was suspended due to accusations some delinquent teenage girls in the facility made against him. The whole story, although not yet proven, made the front pages of the local newspapers and was broadcast on the six and ten o'clock TV news. He was later exonerated, but that never was printed or broadcast!

We all tend to remember the bad stuff we hear on the news about people, without giving a second thought to allegations versus guilt! Even when someone in a certain profession is found guilty, we inadvertently generalize the sin or misdeed to others in the same line of work. At the very least, we become suspicious of entire groups of people. I believe that foster parents are the victims of that kind of thinking right up there with Catholic priests. When one member of the profession is found guilty of an act, the rest become capable of the same act in the eyes of the public.

LAW ENFORCEMENT AND
OTHER PUBLIC OFFICIALS

When we had four delinquent teenage boys in our home,

at first the city police department was cooperative when our boys caused problems. All four of them had backgrounds that included running away from their biological homes. Some of the boys continued their running away patterns while living with us. In the beginning when we would call in a run-away, an officer was dispatched to our home to fill out a report. After many calls to our city police reporting missing kids, the officials there began to treat us more like a nuisance than concerned foster parents. Sometimes we were referred to the boy's county of origin to make the report, other times we were told we had to go down-town in person to file it. One of the officers even implied that it must have been something wrong with us that caused these kids to want to run away. We grew to feel as if the police department didn't want to be bothered with us or our delinquent foster teens. We also felt that they were suspicious of us because of our run-away teens.

The way we resolved reporting run-a-way foster kids was by insisting on having a meeting with a higher up manager at the police department. We explained that because of the number of calls we had to make and the variety of police responses to those calls we had experienced, that we needed to know what procedure they expected from us. In addition, we let them know that they needed to have a uniform procedure response, not something coinciding with the mood-of-the-day. In the end it was resolved that one of us would appear personally at the police station to file run-a-way reports. We followed that procedure knowing it was probably the best we were going to get. We both felt that we were being treated different from other parents in the community who could call and have an officer come to their homes to take similar reports.

The mayor of our city was just the opposite of the police. He was very supportive of foster parents. He came to see me at work one day and told me that he had a minor relative living with him and his wife. He said he had a whole new appreciation for foster parents after taking in a delinquent teen himself. Our mayor made every effort to show foster parents in our community that he valued their work with kids. He is another example of walking in someone else's shoes to know how tough the job is!

While I am on the topic of officials, I want to just say a few things about court officials. Each minor foster child is appointed a guardian ad litem (GAL). In our county they were all attorneys, but I know other areas where volunteers from all walks of life can volunteer and train to be GALS. A GAL is the person who speaks for your foster child in court. He or she represents to the judge what is in the best interest of the minor child. Some GALS do nothing more than read case notes or have a brief phone call with the foster child's case manager. Other GALS talk to the foster parents, the child, and sometimes visit the foster homes.

The bottom line for you is to make sure the GAL on your case knows important information needed to make a sound recommendation to the judge about the future of your foster child. If you have one of those GALS who don't come to you, you need to take the initiative to make sure your opinions and information get on the record. Hopefully your social worker or case manager is including information you provided during your regular meetings together. But, you can't count on that. I know many foster parents don't even have regular meetings with their social workers. Unfortunately even those who do have meetings cannot fully depend on the social worker's court report including all of the valuable information the foster parent provided. The best way to be heard by the court is to attend the hearings on behalf of your foster child in person.

I have been in hundreds of those hearings. In my experience, the judges always asked if a foster parent was present and if the foster parent had anything he or she wished to contribute.

Before leaving this chapter, I want to give you a few more ideas with for surviving among the non-foster and adoptive people in your life:

- As foster parents, we all have to develop thick skin. We have to block suspicious and sarcastic remarks by the public from getting get under it. We are in high profile jobs. Just as law enforcement, the clergy, and others become the targets of suspicion and misunderstanding, so do we.

- Foster and adoptive parents must join together to professionalize their statuses. The first place to start is to join a professional foster care or adoptive parent's association.

- Our foster parent associations must challenge the media to not only sensationalize the negative foster care stories, but give positive credibility to the high majority of foster and adoptive parents who are helping kids.

- We must educate others about what we do as foster and adoptive parents. If some people in our lives are not receptive to our attempts to teach them what we do, then we must have them learn from observation. In addition, foster parents must become public advocates for their profession and for their foster children. One way you can help educate your community is to volunteer to give talks at schools, public service club meetings and church groups about foster parenting. You might even get a few new recruits for your agency to boot!

- In some instances, we have to not care what people think about us. But, be careful in this area because there are some people out there who can hurt you if you take this advice too far. There are people, especially those who are on your child's treatment team, that have a great deal of influence on the outcome of the case. Join them and make sure you have an affect on the case outcome too!

- Give your immediate and extended family time to come around. Mine eventually did. If some of your family members do not get on board with you, they are missing out on a lot. Continue to help kids find their way in life while you try to find a place in your heart that doesn't include the need for approval from everyone in your life.

SUMMARY

As you have come to realize, not everyone will understand or share your desire and motivation to take other people's challenging children into your home. You may be unfairly judged and criticized for choosing to be a foster parent. Without a doubt, as a foster parent, you will live in a glass house where everyone on the outside will be watching you. You and your family will be the subjects of scrutiny by members of your community. Your extended family may not wholeheartedly support you while some of your closest friends may slowly desert you. At the same time you will have new people in your life that you may not have expected there, or whom you do not feel warm and fuzzy towards.

That is just another part of the many challenges of foster parenting. There are, of course, many people who will support you in your efforts to make a better world for abused and neglected children. Along with knowledgeable and helpful professionals in the field, you will include among your friends, other people who are foster parents too. Most important of all, you will have made an impact on the futures of the foster children you have included in your own life.

In order to survive in this profession, you will have to learn how to get the help you need for yourself and for your foster children. You must be able to recognize the people in your life that will be empathetic and supportive to you. To some extent you have to be able to ignore the cynics among your neighbors and friends while at the same time recognize that you can't dismiss the opinions of the professional staff on your child's treatment team. If you plan to be successful in this profession for the long run, you will become an expert at juggling family, friends, and everyone else!

Chapter

5

ABUSE ALLEGATIONS:

PREVENTION

TO SURVIVAL

You might be wondering why I am devoting a whole chapter to preventing and surviving foster parent abuse allegations. When most people think about this topic, they likely associate it with horrible parents who neglect or batter their children. The topic may conger up images of child sexual predators who are either behind bars or living among us as registered sex offenders. We hear about them on TV a lot, especially when a child or teenager goes missing. Most of us have the opinion that child abusers are among the lowest life-forms on the planet.

So how do abuse allegations affect foster parents? The obvious answer to that question from most people is that we are taking care of children who have been neglected, abused or molested. Foster parents may think that dealing with the behaviors resulting from previous abuse might be the only affect on them and their own families. But, there is another big reason for you to spend time reading this section.

You, as a foster or adoptive parent, could be *falsely* accused of abusing your child!

Maybe you have already considered that, or worse yet, you have already been in the position of having to defend yourself against false accusations. For those of you who have not thought about this, or those of you who think it could never happen to you, listen up! Research statistics on false allegations of abuse against foster parents reveals that if a person is a foster parent for seven years, he or she will be investigated for child abuse.

Don't take that to mean that you wouldn't get falsely accused before your seventh year of service. It means that over the long run, a foster parent averages a false child abuse allegation once in every seven years. Your once could be during your first six months as a foster parent. Your one or two times in fourteen years could both happen in your first year. A foster parenting couple in your association could be untouched by abuse allegations for twenty years of service while another couple could be investigated six or seven times during the same period. Incredibly, both of the couples could be completely innocent and parenting in the exact same way!

Some of my most valued foster parent couples in our county's program were the subjects of child abuse allegations. I want you to understand that you can do everything 100% correct and still be a candidate for false child abuse allegations. In the eyes of your agency and law enforcement, you can go overnight from foster parent of the year to a suspect in a child abuse investigation.

You might be asking yourself at this point, "Who in the world would ever put themselves and their own families in this kind of position?" It seems that an informed and sane person would never subject him or herself to becoming a victim of false abuse allegations to a child. Yet there are thousands of foster and adoptive parents who have done just that. Some, because they didn't fully realize the possibility of being falsely accused. Others were willing to go with the higher calling of helping kids in spite of that same possibility.

If I am starting to scare you off, please stay tuned to the rest of this chapter because my objective is to arm you with information and solutions so you can have a long career as a foster parent. Don't allow your fear to overcome your desire to help kids. Keep in mind that in almost any profession now days, people get erroneously accused, sued or fired. My brother is a teacher. He faces the same possibilities of accusations that I do as a foster and adoptive parent. Doctors and nurses are not beyond suspicion, neither are congresspersons, priests or baby-sitters.

I am not going to tell you that I can prevent anyone from becoming a victim of false allegations, but I will say that I can help lower the odds of that happening. There are precautions and preventions you can implement. There are ways to protect yourself. This chapter includes information about how to prevent abuse allegations and what to do if you are actually accused of abusing your foster child during the course of your career.

You should also know that the percentage of foster parents actually found guilty for abusing their foster children is miniscule compared to the general population. The number of substantiated child abuse reports against foster parents is less than one-half of one percent of all substantiated child abuse reports. It is not all doom and gloom, but I want you to fully understand what you are getting yourself into.

AGENCY COMMUNICATION

When I went through the licensing and training process with new foster parents from my county program, I made sure they understood the fact that they could become victims of false child abuse allegations. I explained what the process would be if they indeed were accused of abusing a child in their homes. Child placement agencies, such as the one I worked in, all have procedures they must follow in the event of accusations of child abuse against foster parents.

When investigating allegations against foster parents, agencies must avoid conflicts of interest. That simply means that the social worker or case worker who had been already assigned to the foster family or the foster child could not be the child abuse investigator if a complaint were to be lodged against the foster parents or anyone else living in their home. A social worker or police officer, previously unknown to the alleged foster parent abusers, would be assigned to investigate the child abuse report. The terrifying thing about that is the accused foster parents have zero rapport and credibility in the eyes of the investigator.

Foster parents get a false sense of security from being associated with their child placement agency. They may think that if they indeed become the subjects of a child abuse investigation, that their relationships with social workers and the agency will give them some degree of protection and solace. In fact, it is just the opposite! When an allegation is made against a foster parent, communication between the couple and the agency is nearly shut down.

The foster parents' first line of communication notifying them of an accusation would come from the investigative social worker and/or law enforcement personnel. Their own social worker, who had been assigned to work with them and their foster child, would be instructed not to discuss the abuse allegation with them. Most of the time foster parents find out that they are under investigation by receiving a phone call from the investigative social worker, who had already interviewed the foster child at school. Other foster children placed in the home and the couple's own biological children would have possibly been interviewed at school as well.

It is a horrible shock to be a suspect and also to learn that you don't have the credibility and trust from the agency that you thought you had. It is equally shocking that information about your own case is hard to come by. The investigator is not allowed to reveal the name of the reporter. Foster parents get piece-meal tidbits about what they are suspected of during the process of being questioned about the allegations.

The problem with the line of communication being shut down, and the amount of time it takes for an investigation to be completed, can put a foster family under excruciating stress. Sometimes foster children are removed from the foster parent's home if the authorities feel there is a possibility of any kind of harm to the children. In rare instances, biological children may also be removed and put into protective custody. It is unlikely to have your own birth children removed, but it is very scary to imagine the possibility. In my county's program during my 14 years of employment in child protection and foster care, I do not know of any cases where biological children were taken out of their parents' homes because of allegations by a foster child.

The whole process of investigation through resolution of the child abuse allegations can take up to several weeks. During that time foster parents have no one to turn to. They feel as if they are being treated as criminals and also feel as if they only have each other to talk to about it. It is a frightening and lonely time. Unfortunately, if and when you are accused of abusing a foster child, you will be on your own as far as your foster care agency is concerned. The liability of defending yourself falls directly upon you. Any expenses incurred will not be reimbursed to you when you are found innocent. People who work at your agency will avoid you like a dead fish until the investigation is closed.

Once foster parents are interviewed and the rest of the investigation is completed, the agency and law enforcement decide if they have cause to charge the foster parents with child abuse. Like I said earlier, there are only a small fraction of foster parents who actually get charged with a crime. By far, authorities drop the investigations when the facts are out in the open.

When the investigation is over and you are found innocent, there is still a record of the accusation and investigation in your file at the agency. That is available to all of the foster care social workers. Some social workers at the agency may still judge you to be guilty even though the investigation is closed. Worse yet, the wording that is used by most foster care and police agencies to close the case against you is "abuse unsubstantiated." To me that sounds like the suspect could be guilty, but there just wasn't enough evidence to press charges. When allegations are found to be false, a reasonable person would expect the record to say "False allegations" or "Innocent of Charges." People unfamiliar with you and the false accusation episode could read the file in the future and possibly come to negative conclusions about you.

If law enforcement was involved and you were actually charged with a misdemeanor or a felony, and the case against you was dropped, there would be a record of that as well. The police record would read something like: "charged with misdemeanor (or felony) harm to a child, charges dropped." People such as future employers or adoption agencies could check these public records and read something into the closed case that could prevent you from getting a new job or adopting a child. Now days everyone does background checks!

If you are a foster parent who is hoping to adopt a child in the future, the words "unsubstantiated abuse of a child" in your foster care file could be problematic. Imagine yourself as a social worker investigating the background of a couple who wish to adopt their 3 year-old foster daughter. They have a clean criminal background check, but the county or state foster parent file on the couple shows two unsubstantiated sexual abuse incidents stemming from a former teenage foster daughter. Would you allow them to adopt a 3 year-old girl, who is too young to report sexual abuse. With 'unsubstantiated allegations of sexual abuse,' would you allow the adoption to proceed? The record of the past incident, at the very least, is a huge red flag.

ALLEGATIONS AND THE MEDIA

Remember from chapter 4 how the media loves sensational headlines? God forbid that you are ever involved in a case that becomes the attention of the Channel 5 News or the Daily Gazette! People remember the accusations and charges. They remember the awful details that they read about or see on the news. There are bells and whistles calling attention to every detail that the media is allowed to tell. But, when the case is closed because of unfounded charges or unsubstantiated allegations, the media stays obscenely silent. The only people who hear about your innocence are the ones who make it a point to know. There is usually no huge front page story about a foster parent being found innocent of alleged charges. When there is a miniscule line or two in the news-paper about charges being dropped, the wording of "unsub-stantiated charges" allows the public's negative ideas to linger around! It reminds me of O.J. Simpson. After being charged of murdering his wife and her companion, the world-wide news coverage made O.J. Simpson a household word. Even though he was adjudicated innocent, most of us don't know the details or the truth about what happened. We still think he is a monster who snuffed out his mate.

Another impact is felt by foster parents as the result of the media. Once in a while, you will read a story in the newspaper about a foster or adoptive family who is featured in the human interest section. Or, a local TV station will have a short clip on an admirable couple who have 8 foster and adopted kids with special needs. Most of the good and heartwarming features do not represent the average foster parents. Foster parents having one or two foster children, with both parents holding down fulltime jobs, are not recognized for their equally big hearts and challenging work. Only the sensational stories, on one extreme or the other, receive media coverage.

Although most of us are not in the newspapers or on tele-vision, the foster parents who are depicted by the media, are unfortunately representative of all of us. When a very horrible foster parent story hits the news, the negative images get stuck in people's minds, which makes them suspicious of all foster parents' motives. A recent story about 11 special needs ad-opted children in Ohio planted the image in viewers' minds of foster parents warehousing kids to make lots of money. The ugliness and wrongdoing of two people easily may become generalized to the larger community of foster and adoptive parents.

Media stories about waiting kids are also misrepresentative

of the larger group of kids needing foster homes or waiting to be adopted. Maybe you have viewed a TV advertisement for Big Brothers & Sisters. The ad tries to recruit volunteers to be a big brother or sister to an adorable, normal looking child. Most new foster parents desire foster child placements who resemble the normal children they have seen in the media.

For very good reasons, they want foster children who will blend in with their own families and not cause too much disruption in their lives.

The media does not do justice to the entire group of children needing parents and foster homes. The number of children and teens waiting for foster homes or adoptive placements, with very challenging behaviors and severe emotional problems, is at least ten times the number of 'normal' children. From observations on television or what they read in the papers, many new foster parents have formed images in their minds of nice kids who need placement because their parents have problems. The reality is that the kids have problems too! It is quite an eye-opener for many new foster parents when they discover that normal foster children waiting for placement are few and far between.

THE VULNERABILITY OF FOSTER PARENTS

Children who have been placed in foster care are damaged in emotional ways which affects their behaviors for years, and often for their entire lifetimes.

Foster children have learned coping behaviors such as manipulation and telling lies. They often lose the ability to trust others. They sometimes try to destroy positive relationships with caretakers because of previous multiple abandonments by parents and others. The kids may learn to feel that they are unlovable. When someone shows them love or kindness, they become suspicious or try to sabotage the relationship. Their thinking might be: "I'll hurt you before you hurt me!" That gives them a feeling of control in the relationship. Allen told me that he used to think that way when he was a kid, and continued to think like that way well into his adulthood.

Some of the kids in foster care have learned to be pretty good liars. In fact, the children we take into our homes have usually been victims of some form of child abuse. Our foster children often have graphic detailed memories about what has actually happened to them in their pasts by the hands of people who did abuse them. Coupled with those mentally imprinted horrible memories are the self-protective behaviors they have developed in order to survive. Some of their false accusations can be very convincing when they have actual memories from previous experiences to draw upon. They will use those survival behaviors while placed in foster care.

Foster children may tell lies about their birth parents and their foster parents. They may also tell their social worker one story and the foster parents another story. We had a teenage foster daughter who told the social worker things about us and our home that did not put us in a very good light. Out of the other side of her mouth, behind her social worker's back, she said things that the social worker supposedly said and did that made us suspicious. When Allen and I sat down with the social worker and talked about all of it, we found out that our foster daughter was duping all of us. It seems that she liked to start trouble and watch everyone else duke it out. I compare it to an arsonist lighting a fire to watch it burn. Once we were on to her, the social worker, Allen and I made it a point to speak to each other and compare notes! The three of us had a much better relationship once we eliminated our foster daughter as the middle man and unofficial messenger!

Another way foster parents are vulnerable is that social workers and other professionals have been trained that children are honest. Back in the old days, social work students were taught in college that children don't lie. There is still much of that kind of thinking among foster care social work staff. Children have been historically viewed as innocent victims with no motivation to distort the truth. They have had more credibility in the eyes of social workers and law enforcement staff than their parents and foster parents. Fortunately that kind of thinking is beginning to change. Most social workers have caught kids in lies and they are beginning to understand the self-preservation reasoning behind children's motivations to distort the truth.

In today's foster care world, children are not always honest and should not be believed unconditionally. Please do not misunderstand me. Child abuse is terrible. All known incidents of neglect, physical violence, sexual abuse and emotional abuse inflicted upon children should be reported to child protection authorities. The workers who are at the receiving end of child abuse reports should and do take them all seriously. The investigators do not know an unfounded allegation from an actual child abuse incident, whether the alleged abuse originated against biological parents, foster parents, friends of the family or complete strangers. All abuse reports must be looked into. Innocent children do need protection, but sometimes innocent foster parents get caught in the crossfire.

The children who are placed in foster care come from very unstable and hazardous family situations. A great majority of their birth parents are involved in activities that entangle them with the law. Their parents may be involved in one or more of these activities: Illegal drug use; Illegal drug sales; Welfare fraud; Petty theft; Domestic Violence; Child abuse;

Child neglect; Child sexual abuse; Burglary; Alcoholism; Re-occurring Disorderly Conduct. That is just to mention some of the illegal things that go on in some of our foster children's biological families. Many of our foster children's family members would stoop to lies and false accusations to get what they want or to get even with society. Foster children coming from these environments may have observed and learned the same scruples and tactics that were employed by their parents.

The majority of our foster children's mothers are single parents. Many of the moms are mentally unstable or below average intelligence. Men come and go in their lives, often taking advantage of the women and mistreating their children. For their own self-preservation, these kids learn to lie. If mom's boyfriend might beat the snot out of a child for spilling his milk, the child will learn to deny the deed. In our house, we have observed kids lying about stealing cookies after being caught with their hands in the cookie jar.

Children who are being abused and neglected still love their parents. Sometimes they lie to authorities to protect mom or dad from the law. In spite of their bad circumstances at home, kids don't want their parents to be taken away from them. They may tell lies to try and keep their families intact. Some foster children may go to great extremes to be able to go back to their abusive birth homes.

Incredible as that sounds, foster parents have to always remember that their foster children love their real parents. Kids sometimes make up stories to try and put their foster parents in a bad light. Their reasoning is that if the foster parents are seen as bad by the agency, then the social worker will let them go back home.

Birth parents of foster children also have been known to make false accusations against foster parents. I have worked with a few mothers who called social services and refused to take their sons or daughters back to the foster homes after their home visits. They would allege that the foster parents abused their children.

In one case, I had a 3 year-old girl in a foster home. The foster parents had an 8 year-old daughter of their own, and two other foster children under the age of 5. They had been foster parents for our agency for 14 years and had provided care for over 50 other children without incident over that amount of time. The foster mom stayed home full-time to provide care for the children. We always thought of that couple as among the best of our group. One Sunday night when their 3 year-old foster daughter was supposed to return home to them after a weekend with her birth mother, they received a very disturbing phone call.

The birth mother phoned an hour after she was scheduled to bring her daughter back and told the foster mother that she was not coming. She accused the foster parents of bruising the child's buttocks. She informed them that she was calling social services (that would be me at the time) to pick the child up. It turned out that the child did have new black and blue marks on her backside.

The foster mom said she had bathed the child just before sending her home for the weekend with her birth mother and did not notice any marks on her. She suspected that the girl's mother had inflicted those marks on her own child and then tried to cover it up by blaming it on the foster parents.

The situation was resolved by questioning the child. She wouldn't say that her mother did it, but she told me that her foster mother and father never spanked her. On the flip side, her birth mother had put bruises on her butt in the past. I returned the child to the foster home. She appeared happy to go back there. I worked it out with her foster mother that I would come to their house to and inspect the child myself, right before she left for anymore weekend visits with her mom. I also had the home visits supervised for quite a long time into the future to insure the little girl's safety with her mother.

The birth mother in that case eventually lost any enthusiasm she had to meet the conditions set by the judge. Her requests for visits dwindled away. When I tried to set them up with her, she was either too busy or didn't return my calls. The child was later adopted by that foster family after the birth mother's parental rights were terminated.

As a foster parent, you can't predict or stop a birth parent from abusing a child during a home visit, just as you can't predict or stop a birth parent from making false allegations against you. You can't prevent kids from fabricating stories either. Without any wrong-doing on your own part, you can become a suspect or a party of interest in a child abuse investigation.

Another thing I've witnessed happening is teenagers thinking their foster parents are too strict. I have had kids tell me how cruel and mean their foster parents were. From the foster parent's sides of the stories, the kids thought they were mean because the foster parents were enforcing reasonable rules and curfews. Foster teens sometimes blow these things out of proportion in the hope that they will be placed in different foster homes, who might not have as strict of rules.

A lot of foster teenagers are savvy and streetwise. They have learned unscrupulous ways to get what they want. Foster parents raising teenagers have to become just a savvy as their kids in order to understand the motivations behind their behaviors. A foster parent who is too trusting and wanting to believe a foster teenager unconditionally can quickly become vulnerable.

As I discussed earlier, a foster child may behave in one way while interacting with dad, and behave totally differently while interacting with mom. Remember that it is possible for each parent to see a different child. Foster boys are often angry with their absent fathers and will take that anger out on other men, especially foster dads. Foster daughters will sometimes try to get between a foster mother and father by attempting to win over dad's affections, thus taking away some of mom's power.

It is critical to understand the underlying motivations behind foster children's behaviors. Even more important, foster moms and dads have to stay on the same channel when parenting these kids! There are ways for fostering couples to work together to lessen the chances of false abuse allegations from foster children.

If you are already a seasoned foster parent, think about some of the mental health labels our foster children carry. They are often diagnosed as Borderline Personality Disorder, Oppositional Defiant Disorder and/or Attachment Disorder. Did you know that lying and making false allegations are symptoms in all of these diagnoses? The children themselves often don't know why they do what they do. Foster parents must be informed and educated about their foster children's mental illnesses and their symptoms. Ignorance on caretaker's parts about children's disorders, and their resulting behaviors, definitely makes for a very vulnerable situation for both the children and their foster parents!

Foster parents have another area of vulnerability that we sometimes don't think about. We are licensed to be foster parents and are obliged to obey the rules of our licensing agency.

Foster parents are held to higher standards than the rest of the parenting community. Something that is viewed as non-abusive in a biological family may be viewed as abusive in a foster family. Sending a child to bed without supper is an example where a birth family would not be challenged but a foster parent would be breaking the licensing rules. Spanking is another area. As biological parents, we can spank our kids without getting into too much trouble, but it is against the rules to spank our foster children. In fact, in some states foster parents are not even allowed to spank their own biological children when there are foster children in the same home. Foster parents have strict licensing rules they must follow to the letter. As a result, they are held to much higher public scrutiny.

The intense scrutiny that foster parents experience can be fueled by their foster children's negative behaviors in the community. Foster parents often get judged unfairly by their children's deeds. For example: Last year our adopted son got practically straight F's in all of his classes in high school. Even though we supervised him doing his homework, he often didn't bother to turn it in. A couple of his teachers thought that we were parents who just didn't care about our son's grades. They did not realize that our son came to us with severe emotional problems and they did not understand the progress he has made since he was placed with us. At the beginning of this school year we were invited to a conference about our son. He has tremendously improved his grades and has gotten to know the vice-principal. After meeting us, the vice-principal told us that he had a different kind of picture in his mind about the kind of parents we were, until he actually met us in person.

Foster children often stand out in social situations. Other

people do not understand the damage that was done to them before they were placed in foster care. When these kids react to situations based on what they learned from their experiences prior to foster care, frequently the foster parents get blamed for their behaviors.

STORIES FROM MY HOUSE

I'll start out by sharing what has happened to Allen and me during our 14 years as foster and adoptive parents. We have had our share of problems with false allegations, but the bright side of our story is that we survived the ordeals and are both here to share our stories with you. Best of all, we are enjoying our three adopted boys, who were formerly our foster children. They are the end of the line for us as far as adoption and foster care. We have seen them through emotional problems, challenging behaviors, poor academic performance, and rejection. In spite of all their setbacks in early life, all of them have made tremendous progress and are getting ready to launch into their own independent lives.

Jake, 18, is actually going to graduate from high school next year after a few rough years of terrible grades and not caring about school. He plans on joining the Air Force. Jared, 17, has raised his grades from a year ago of D's and F's to A's and B's. He is learning to restore wrecked cars while working side-by-side on garage projects with Allen. He will have learned enough about auto body work to obtain a job in that field after graduation. Jamie, 11, is on the honor roll at school so far this year, except for a C in conduct. He is the same age as our granddaughter! (He is the bomber I talked about in chapter 3.)

Today, we are doing OK and don't have any major regrets over our decisions to foster and adopt. If anyone were to ask us if we would do it all over again, we would answer, "yes." But, we were investigated for alleged child abuse and if the same question was asked during those times, we may have had a negative answer. Fortunately time has left us with more of the good memories and has allowed some of our wounds inflicted by false allegations to heal.

We were falsely accused of sexual abuse to a fifteen year old boy during our second year of foster parenting. At the time, we had four teenaged boys placed in our home. All of them had drug and alcohol issues along with delinquency, theft, and truancy. Their behaviors had become so out of control that their biological parents couldn't handle them.

One of the boys, Ben (not his real name) accused both Allen and me of strip searching him. To understand where this charge came from, I'll have to tell you more about Ben's treatment plan.

We had a plan in writing with our social worker that would prevent Ben from bringing contraband into our home. We had already taken away items such as matches, pot, cigarettes, knives, numb chucks, brass knuckles and throwing stars. In order to protect ourselves and feel safe in our own home, our treatment plan for Ben included searches for harmful objects whenever he returned from a home visit.

Several times dangerous items had gotten past us because Ben would sneak things into our home hidden in his under-wear, jacket lining or shoes. After discussing our fears about this with our social worker, she came up with a plan that made us feel safer. We were allowed to search the Ben when he entered the house after home visits.

According to our social worker's treatment plan, Ben would be asked to give us his shoes and jacket the minute he walked into our house. His mother was to be with him and she was required to stay until we went through the rest the clothes Ben was wearing. If she refused to stay, she would have to take him back home with her. Ben would be instructed by Allen to go in the bathroom and undress to his underwear, then hand his clothes out the door. Allen, while standing in the hallway with Ben's mother, would check his clothes for contraband, then hand them back in to Ben. Allen would watch him put them back on. He had to be observed dressing because he could potentially hide a knife or something in the bathroom and then put it back in his pocket when getting dressed again. His mother would be in the hallway adjoining the bathroom. This procedure to search Ben was included in a written treatment plan with our social worker and the placing agency.

One day our other three boys came home from high school and told us they had all been interviewed by a police officer and a social worker. They said that they were asked questions like, "Do Allen or Mary ever touch you inappropriately?" or "Has anyone ever performed a strip search on you?" The boys remarks to us about being questioned at school were the first indications we had that we were under some kind of suspicion.

We called our social worker immediately. She said we were being investigated for performing strip searches on Ben. She indicated that at the time she could not discuss it any further than repeating the charges.

In our naivety about the possibility of false charges, Allen and I overlooked a huge red flag in Ben's case history. A year earlier he had accused a counselor, at a group home where he was placed, of sexually abusing him. All we knew about that incident was that the charges against the counselor were dropped. We allowed Ben to come into our home as a foster placement anyway, believing that our credibility with our agency would protect us. We assumed that if he accused us of any wrong doing, based on that credibility and on his past actions, that our agency would quickly come to our defense.

We later found out that the charges Ben made before coming to our house regarding that counselor were ridiculous! He accused his counselor of drugging and raping him. He said he was knocked out after consuming a Hershey Bar that had been injected with sleeping medication. When he woke up he was in a different place and his counselor was having sex with him.

Ben had a long history of lying and dishonesty. The charges against his counselor were absurd, but were still investigated. It was all dropped, but the detailed information about that prior incident was left out of Ben's case history.

Ben was diagnosed as 'out of touch with reality.' He was on psychotropic medications for his mental illness. We knew that he made up stories that were far-fetched and that he told his stories as if he believed they really happened. Prior to the allegations against us, we felt assured by the agency that they would stand with us if he ever made anything up about us.

Ben was from the county next to ours, so the investigation was done by that county. A detective, who didn't know us and who didn't know Ben's history, was put in charge of the investigation. It took him a month to complete his inquiries and close the investigation. In his process he had talked to us, Ben, Ben's mother (also mentally ill), teachers at school, our social worker, Ben's therapist, and all of our children.

During the month that the investigation was open, Allen and I first went through shock that we were under suspicion of sexual abuse followed by feelings of terror at the prospect of people believing Ben. There was nothing our social worker could do to stop the investigation. We had no idea of what else Ben might fabricate or accuse us of.

The only thing that made us feel that we could survive the whole ordeal of being falsely accused was the fact that we knew we followed his treatment plan to the letter and never crossed any boundaries that would support the accusations that Ben had made. We had only each other to talk to about our situation. We lived for a month in deep fear of the outcome after learning that we didn't have the credibility we thought we had!

After waiting for what seemed like a year to us, but in reality was about 30 days, we received a letter from the investigating detective stating that there was not enough evidence to prove we had sexually abused Ben. The case was being closed as "unfounded charges." The letter advised us that strip searches were illegal and suggested that having Ben undress in front of Allen could lead to future investigations and that could be construed as a strip search.

We decided that we didn't want to keep Ben in our home under those circumstances. We were told by the detective that he couldn't be searched and at the same time our social worker insisted that we could still do the same treatment plan and continue just as we had in the past. We felt that we would be setting ourselves up for future investigations if we allowed Ben to stay, or that he would hurt someone in our house if we couldn't search him for contraband.

Before the agency had time to move Ben, he did something to seal his own fate. He and another boy stole a car and were both put in jail. The decision was lifted from us. Ben was sent away to a juvenile detention facility. In retrospect, I now believe that Ben should have never been placed in a foster home. From the beginning, he was a candidate for a more intensive and restrictive placement! In my head I knew that from the beginning, but my emotional side had convinced me to give him a chance. Our treatment foster care agency had accepted Ben for a placement when they should have known that his behaviors were beyond what a foster family could handle.

That whole experience taught us that foster parents can become subjects of child abuse investigations even when the child has a history of making false allegations and is a habitual liar. As ridiculous as the Hershey Bar injection story was, it was still investigated. We were investigated even though we were doing exactly what was in our foster child's written treatment plan. Finally and most importantly, we were guilty of not heeding information in the child's case history and questioning items that pointed toward caretaker allegations. Hindsight taught us that we should have never taken Ben into our home in the first place.

About 2 years after the whole thing with Ben, we were almost investigated again. We were in the process of adopting our daughter, Cindy (not her real name). She had a school counselor at her elementary school who also wanted to adopt her. Cindy was considered special needs because of her emotional and behavioral problems. The state social worker had already licensed us and approved us for adoption when the school counselor, Mrs. X, came into the picture.

At the time, in addition to Cindy, we had our daughter, Brenna, sons, John, Jake, and Jared in our home along with Melissa, our foster daughter. Mrs. X knew all of our kids. We lived in a very small town where everyone knew everyone else.

One day, soon after Cindy's adoption was finalized, we received a call from the state adoption social worker. She told us that there was a complaint filed against us by someone at the elementary school. It stated that: 1) Our children were all too thin, and that we must not be feeding them properly. 2) We had locks on our cupboards, refrigerator, freezer, and pantry. 3) The children were locked in their rooms at night. 4) We had video cameras in all of the bedrooms.

Of course, none of that was true. Once again, we thought we were about to be the center of an investigation. But this time the state social worker and our agency social worker went to bat for us. They called a meeting with Mrs. X and the school principal. That meeting resulted in the principal and Mrs. X being invited to inspect our home themselves. Mrs. X was angry that she was not considered a candidate to adopt Cindy. She continued to question all of our children at school about how they were being treated in our home.

As a result of her constant vigilance and erroneous suspicions, Mrs. X ended up being instructed by her principal to have absolutely no contact with any of our children. She was looking for something to go wrong and trying very hard to get some kind of negative goods on us. In that instance, other professionals stood by us and helped us get that misguided school counselor out of our lives!

We have another adopted daughter who caused us a great deal of stress and heart ache. I will call her Joann to keep her identity confidential. She was removed from her biological parents home along with an older sister and brother when she was eight years old. She was a beautiful and talented girl. She got straight A's in school with very little effort. We adopted her at the age of 12 when she had been in our home as a foster daughter for about a year. She was in the school band, debate club, dance, and drama clubs. But along with her intelligence and talent, she had a very disturbed side. Every time she was in a social setting, she got into some kind of trouble.

When she was fifteen, she went on a school band trip to a college campus in our neighboring state. After her part of the competition was over, she took off and was later found with some college boys in their dorm room. The school banned her from participating on any future field trips. She became more and more defiant as time went on. I believe that she was preoccupied about her birth mother, who was a drug addict and stripper.

One night she ran away by exiting out her bedroom window. She was missing for four days. We later found out that during that time she was at a friend's house. The friend's mother let her stay because Joann made up a story about being mistreated at our house. She and her friend went on the internet and looked up Joann's biological mother. She called her mother and gave her a big story about how terrible it was to live with us. Her birth mother called our county social services and reported us as child abusers.

Joann's birth mother actually drove 120 miles to our town and picked Joann up and delivered her to social services. We were contacted by an investigative social worker the same day. The worker insisted at meeting me at the police station rather than coming out to our house. When I got there, I was the one who had to defend myself, rather than my daughter, who had run away and lied to everyone. After the social worker felt comfortable that we were not abusing Joann, she allowed me to take her back home. Before we walked out of the police station, she handed Joann her business card and told her to call anytime she felt threatened by us. It made me feel as though the social worker really didn't believe my account of the events and that our 15 year-old adopted daughter was a fragile, vulnerable victim, rather than an out-of-control teenager!

From that day forward, both Allen and I worried about

what she would come up with next! We were asked to have ongoing contact with social services so they could monitor us and provide family counseling. All of a sudden, instead of providing services, I became a client! That was a hard pill to swallow! Through no fault of our own and because of the actions of our delinquent adopted daughter, our family was labeled as dysfunctional and in need of social services. This teenager had turned our lives upside-down. I could write a whole other book about our experiences with Joann!

The worst part about the whole situation was that I had a relationship with that county child protection agency. At the time I was the county foster care coordinator in the next county over. I had loaned foster homes to that agency and had taught foster care and adoption classes to their foster parents and social workers. My status and prior credibility with them was completely ignored. Our family was forced to work with a 22 year-old first-year social worker, who had no children of her own, and who thought she knew better than we did how to parent our delinquent daughter. What an eye-opener! Needless to say, Allen and I celebrated when Joann turned 18! It was a very long three years.

Like I said earlier, a foster parent couple can go from foster parents of the year to becoming clients of a child protection agency, overnight, without ever knowing what hit them! But, before you decide to bail out, there are some things I am going to tell you that will help.

WHAT YOU CAN DO
TO LESSEN THE ODDS OF FALSE ALLEGATIONS

I have to start this section by telling you that you can do everything I recommend here and still be falsely accused at some time in the future. But, there are things you can do to lessen the odds of that happening and actions you can take now to protect yourself in the future. If I knew what we were going to be in for, I certainly would have done some things differently. My husband and I really felt like quitting when we were right in the thick of some of our allegation experiences. We hung in there for our kids and I want to help you be able to do the same. You need to be prepared in advance for the possibility that a foster child might make a false allegation against you. Please read and carefully consider the following preventative measures:

1. Before you accept any new foster child placement into your home, get as much information as possible about the child.

    - Learn about the child's previous behaviors including lying, destructiveness, combativeness, ability to get along with others, eating patterns, sleeping patterns, social skills, school performance, and other behaviors.

    - Ask if the child was ever a victim of sexual abuse. If the child was a victim, there is a greater chance that he or she will victimize someone else. You have to protect other vulnerable children in your home. This applies to boys as well as girls. In addition to protecting other children in your home, you have to think about protecting yourself as well. When children with sexual abuse histories make allegations, they have very graphic memories to draw upon in the event they make false allegations against you. Have your social worker give you the information in writing.

    - Find out if the child had previous foster care or relative placements. If so, why did the placements fail? Ask to speak with the former caretakers or foster parents to find out exactly what went wrong.

- Has the child ever made false allegations against anyone? If so, how was it investigated and resolved? Get the details in writing. If the same type of false allegations are made against you, you will have something that establishes a pattern of behavior. You will also know how believable the story was and what measures were taken during the previous investigation.

- Has the child been sexually active or promiscuous? If so, you will have to have a plan to not let the child be alone in your home with a member of the opposite sex. You will also encounter a higher chance of each parent 'seeing a different child.'

- Inquire about the child's biological family. What will be the degree of difficulty working with them? Does the child have visits with them? If so, are they supervised? By whom? What is your own role? Has the birth family made false accusations in the past?

- What medications is the child on? For what reason? What are the possible side affects? Get the complete medical history.

- Will the child be in special education classes? Will riding the school bus be a problem? Has the child had suspensions or expulsion from school in the past?

- Does the child have a history of abusing animals?

- Has the child ever started a fire?
- Will the child need supervision beyond the normal level appropriate for his or her age level? (I do not leave my 18 year-old and my 17 year-old home alone. Most parents could trust a child that age home alone.)

2. Decide if the child being offered for placement is within your capabilities to parent. (Remember, that is where we went wrong with Ben!) Can you give everyone in your home, including the new foster child, enough time and attention? Can you meet everyone's individual needs? How will the new kid fit in with your own biological children and other foster children? Are you putting anyone (including yourself) at risk of being harmed emotionally or physically?

3. Say "no" to accepting a placement if you feel the child will not work out in your home. Lots of foster parents are afraid to say no, thinking that if they don't help out the agency that they will not get offered future placements. That is not true. Agencies get overwhelmed with kids needing placements. They need you. If you are unable to accept a placement for whatever reason you have, another offer from the agency will soon follow. You will make a worse impression on the agency if you accept a child you can't handle and request to have the child moved again early on. You also have to think about the amount of added stress and disruption to you and the rest of your family that getting in over your head will certainly create.

4. From the first day of the placement until the day your foster child leaves your home, keep your own

case records. The rest of the other professionals on your child's treatment team all document the case. You must too! Documentation could clear up or explain something that initiated a false allegation. You may need to provide an investigative worker with specifics. By documenting events the day they actually occur, you won't have to rely on your memory.

- Use a bound notebook, the kind that shows if pages have been torn out, to keep a record for each foster child in your home. (If you use a spiral notebook or the computer, pages could be torn out or records changed. For legal purposes, a bound book is more permanent.) Have a separate notebook for each foster child.

- Write down anything out of the ordinary that happens. If your child falls down and skins his knee, write that down. How did it occur? What did you do about it? How did the child react? Make sure to include the date and time of the incident. So many things happen with kids that we can tend to forget incidents or blur them together in our memories. If we don't write things down, they become lost or distorted.

- If your child tells lies, write that down. Leave out your feelings about it and include only the facts and circumstances. Write down how you handled the situation.

- Write down how your child behaves both before and after parental home visits. Include comments that seem out of the ordinary made by the child and the biological parents. Document the time the child left your home and the time he returned.

- Keep track of absences from school, contacts with school personnel, school performance and behaviors. Include the reasons for absences and other contacts.

- Document all contacts you have with your case worker and counselors. Include the topics of the conversation, where your meeting took place, time of day, date, suggestions made by the worker, and any important information you provided.

- Write down things that 'trigger' behaviors with your foster child. Triggers are memories, sounds, voices, songs, pictures, and other events that ignite undesirable behaviors in foster children. Remember the song on the car radio that Roger heard. He went into a sullen and withdrawn state upon hearing a country western song on the car radio. We later found out that it reminded him of the way his birth dad sang.

- In general, write down anything that you want to share with the social worker or other team members. You have the most contact with, and knowledge about your foster child. You are the one who spends 24 hours a day with him. You cannot possibly remember everything that is important for the other team members to know. Write it down and date it as soon as it occurs!

5) Make sure you know and understand all of your agency's licensing rules and regulations. Sometimes foster parents get into trouble with their agencies by breaking foster care licensing rules. For instance, if

your state's rules say that you must keep all medications, cleaning supplies, and insecticides locked up, and a foster child becomes seriously ill from ingesting one of them, you would be in serious trouble. Know and review the rules. Never bend them or slack off from them!

6) Develop family rules and post them for all family members to see. An example of some rules from our house:

- Only one person is allowed in the bathroom at one time. The bathroom door must remain closed while in use. No one is allowed to barge in on anyone else.

- Bedroom doors must be closed while getting dressed. At all other times, the doors should be open.

- Boys and girls are not allowed in each other's bedrooms. Mom will not be alone with a boy in his room, and dad will not be alone with a girl in her room.

It is important not to have too many rules, but the rules you have should be designed with everyone's safety in mind, including your own!

7) Maintain clear communication with your child's treatment team. Ask for help when behaviors arise that you don't know how to handle. If you have concerns that your child's needs are not being met, insist that the team gets together to remedy the situation.

8) Maintain a cordial and professional working relationship with all of the treatment team members. Extend that to include the child's birth parents.

9) Prepare in advance in case you are ever falsely ac-

cused of child abuse. Have a plan that includes selecting an attorney who has defended similar cases in the past. When and if you are accused of abusing a foster child, you will be in a state of turmoil. It will be hard to think clearly. By having an attorney and support people in mind, you will not have to make those difficult choices while in the primary shock and fear stages of your case.

HELP FOR FOSTER PARENTS
WHO HAVE BEEN ACCUSED OF CHILD ABUSE

Remember that the statistics tell us that if you continue foster parenting for the long run, at some point you will most likely be falsely accused of abusing a child or breaking a licensing rule. If and when a social worker or investigator approaches you about an allegation of abuse, it is natural to feel upset and frightened. I remember feeling shock followed by the feeling that the floor was sinking! For the first few days, it was all I could think about. Allen and I felt that we had no one to talk to about it. I want to share some survival tips you can use if you ever find yourself in a position of having to defend yourself against a false allegation.

Start out by remembering that you are innocent. The proof that would be needed to find you guilty is not there if you didn't do anything. That fact alone helped me stay calmer during our investigative processes. Above all else, maintain your professionalism. It is very understandable that you might feel like blowing up at someone, but feeling like that and doing it are two different things. You must control your anger, or you will look guilty. Anyone wearing your shoes would be upset and angry too. You have a right to be so, but don't take it out on anyone else. This might take some real work, but staying cool is absolutely a must.

Become focused on understanding the allegation and the procedures that will follow. Ask for the allegation in writing. Make sure you understand the time-line of the investigation. You have a right to a written finding at the end. You also have a right to request a fair hearing if you disagree with the investigator's final decision. Check with your local agency to know how soon you must file an appeal.

Make your foster child available for interviews. Don't drill the child or discuss the alleged incident prior to the social worker's interviews. The social worker will most likely ask both you and the child if you discussed the alleged incident. She will ask the child if you suggested something to say about it.

Take some comfort in the fact that children have a hard time keeping their lies straight. It has been my experience that when kids are asked to tell about a false allegation again and again, the story changes slightly each time it is told. You can be sure that the investigator will ask the child many times and in many different ways to repeat the allegations. Usually children who are lying trip themselves up. On the other hand, you will be telling the truth and have your facts straight.

There may be more than one agency involved in the investigation. If you are a foster parent alleged to have abused a foster child, licensed by a private agency, your county child protection agency or your state agency will certainly be involved as well. If you are charged with a foster care licensing violation, it may be only the agency who licensed you that will be investigating.

If you are alleged to have committed a crime against a child, a county or state prosecutor may be involved. For instance, if a child accused you of sexually abusing her, and there was enough convincing evidence to support that allegation, the case would be turned over to the district attorney's office. The ensuing investigation would take precedence over a private or public child welfare agency's case.

Understand your rights and hire legal counsel. In criminal cases, it is the state's burden to prove beyond a reasonable doubt that you have committed a crime. If you have been accused of a foster care licensing violation, then the agency will make a finding which you have a right to appeal. As I stated earlier, make sure you understand the appeal process and the time constraints that apply in your agency as well as your state.

Seek out other foster parents who have been through the same experience. In most areas there are foster parents support groups you can join. There are also some internet resources you can contact for support. On your computer search, type in key words such as 'foster parent abuse allegations' or 'foster parent support groups.' You may feel like isolating yourself, but don't do that. Others who have walked in your shoes before you can be very helpful and comforting.

Try to keep the whole ordeal in prospective. Allegations against foster parents are made everyday somewhere in the country. Remember the fact that there is only a minuscule number of reports that actually lead to licensing revocation or prosecution. If you are innocent of the allegations, it will come out. In the mean time, try and go on with life as usual. Most foster parents have to go on parenting their children during the investigation. Thousands of people before you have been through the same process and are still out there providing excellent care for foster children.

When the process is over, try to put it behind you. That

may sound easier to accomplish than it actually is. Foster parents who have been falsely accused of abusing their foster children feel scarred and publicly humiliated, not to mention angry. Try your very best to put it in the past. In our own case, we had to develop thick skin and to be able to not care what other people thought about us. You and your higher power are your only judges. When you know that you are innocent, it doesn't matter in the long run what other people think. Time heals our wounds and allows us to reframe our unpleasant experiences.

I will not try to white-wash the feelings that we have been through. The old saying, 'Once bitten = twice shy' certainly applies to anyone who has been falsely accused of child abuse. If you cannot get over your negative feelings about the whole thing, and you feel paranoid about future similar charges, you probably should quit foster parenting. The fact that you could be falsely accused again is hanging over your head. If you can't live with that possibility, you will not be able to affectively parent difficult foster children.

If you decide that foster parenting is your call in life and you choose to continue, like we did, carefully read and re-read the previous section on preventions you can take. Being accused is not the end of the world. The whole process is difficult, but you do learn to be more selective in the placements you take and better educated in the ways you can protect yourself!

Chapter

6

HINDSIGHT

If I knew then what I know now, would I do it all over again? The answer is not a simple 'yes.' I know that Allen and I made some huge impacts on our foster and adopted children's lives. Most of them haven't come right out and told us that, nevertheless, we know it's true. I know we would have done some things differently if we possessed the knowledge and skills we have today.

Some of our kids have learned that they can trust people, and some of them still have been unable to accomplish that. We have exposed them all to different kinds of life-styles than those they had been privy to in their pasts. They each have had the chance to see that the world has hope and opportunities. A couple of our children, who are grown up, are struggling through life. We question ourselves over how we could have better helped them, but still know that we did everything we could for them. We celebrate our successes and try not to be too hard on ourselves for our mistakes.

Allen is a testament to the fact that his world was opened up widely by his experiences in his foster homes. His biological mother lived in the run-down welfare section of Milwaukee. As the result of an absent father and mentally ill mother, his view of the world would have been much harsher and narrower had he not been exposed to the life-styles of his many foster parents through his formative years. He still has memories, both good and bad, about his foster care experiences. He is planning on telling his story in an upcoming book called Allen's Story.

As a couple, sometimes foster parenting felt too hard for us to continue. There were a few kids who didn't work out in our home. It was hard to let go of them, even though we knew they needed more than we could offer them. Some social workers didn't understand how difficult our job was and other social workers were like our right hands. There were people in the community and at my work who didn't understand our motives for taking on all of those tough kids and who criticized us. At the same time there were many people who admired the job we were doing. Sometimes our own family didn't understand why we wanted all of those kids in our lives, but we persevered in our mission to help kids. Most of our family members eventually came around.

During times that I felt like quitting, I tried to think of the story that Allen told me about wanting to stay married to the same person for 25 years, just like his foster parents had done. I think of that little boy who saw hope for his own future, and who decided that day, he wanted to be like the Otto's in Thiensville Wisconsin. Foster care made a huge difference for him. I am thankful for the fact that Allen choose me to live that dream with. I hope that we have inspired all of our children to fulfill their dreams by our examples.

I had the good fortune today to speak with a former foster parent from Shiocton Wisconsin. His name is Peter Lutz. When Pete first became a foster parent, he was single. He helped me forge the way in Outagamie County Wisconsin for single foster and adoptive parents. Pete was a farmer at the time. He had the ability, especially during Wisconsin's harsh winters, to parent 24 hours a day if needed.

After being a single foster parent for a little over one year, and taking in several children as foster kids, Pete decided he wanted to adopt a child. At the time he was foster dad to 12 year-old Jonathon. Pete wanted to be Jon's forever dad. It was a tough process for both Peter and Jon. Back then, the State of Wisconsin had not yet approved adoptions for very many single dads! In addition to that, Pete had just turned 49.

Pete and I laughed on the phone reminiscing over times when our foster and pre-adoptive kids caused us grief and heartaches! He said, "I can laugh now thinking about the times I was out on the porch waiting for the police to come and talk to Jon." The times that were unbearable when we were raising our kids, now seem funny. Isn't it remarkable what hindsight does for us?

Pete got married the same year Jon's adoption was finalized. He, his wife, Diane, and Jonathan all live together now. Jon has graduated from high school and works full-time as a truck driver. The three of them are all planning a great family vacation this year to celebrate Jon's graduation. Peter told me that without a doubt he would do it all over again!

John and Liz Wiesner are foster parents I have know for years. They live in the rural Hortonville Wisconsin area. John is a self-employed insurance agent and Liz works full-time with him in the office. They got married to each other late in life after both had raised their biological kids to adulthood.

Both of them had a deep desire to help kids. I licensed them as foster parents in Outagamie County Wisconsin. They started out taking in very difficult teenaged boys, many of whom no one else wanted. Eventually, Liz's son, Tim Schmalz, and his Wife, Kathy, also became foster parents. That made the Weisner's both foster parents and foster grandparents at the same time.

Tim and Kathy Schmalz went on to adopt three of their foster children. That turned Liz and John into legal grandparents of the kids. I had dinner with the whole gang last summer in Appleton Wisconsin. It felt great to have been a part of that wonderful family again. When I asked all four of the adults if they would do it all over again, this is what they said:

Liz: "I would do it all over again. My health is not the best, and that is the reason we stopped foster parenting about two years ago. But, definitely the good times out weighed the bad!" She went on to tell me that their first foster son, Adam, asked them to host his wedding this fall at their home. They will have 25 guests including Adam's biological family.

John: "I too, would do it all over again. The impact we had on some of the most difficult kids is too great a reward to not do it! I would want to choose some of the same social workers we had before." He told me that he had some great social workers that he would like to have back if they ever became foster parents again. I know that there are a few teens that Liz and John fostered that still think of them both as another set of parents. This is a couple who continue to give to the kids they cared for. They are still very connected to many of their foster children and grandchildren.

Tim: "I would definitely do it all over again. I think the most rewarding part of being a foster parent for me is hearing from our former kids that we made a difference in how they live their lives today. It is important to me that we had an influence on them."

Kathy: "I would do it again, but I think I would have more caution regarding the kids we took. Most often when we were asked to accept a child into our home, we made that decision based more on our emotions than on rationalizations. Maybe in the long run that made us more successful with the kids we had. I do believe more cautious decisions would have reduced the chaos created in our lives. I love each and every one of them, even the ones that were not a successful match for us. Each child held a separate reward. It was up to me to recognize their gift to me."

Allen told me that he would do it all over again too. He values our experiences with all of our kids and enjoys our very large family. He said that he knows how it feels to be a foster child, and that knowledge motivated him to survive some of the challenges we faced. He had a connection with our kids that enabled him to feel their pain and fears. I know that our three boys who are still at home, Jake 18, Jared 17 and Jamie 11, look up to him and think of him as their 'real dad.' All three of them still hug us every night before they go to bed.

The bottom line is that I would do it all over again, but I wish I knew then what I know now. That could be said for a lot of jobs and life-styles. For me, sharing the information that I have learned and observed through my years as a foster care social worker and foster/adoptive parent, is a way I hope to help other foster and adoptive parents have more foresight and knowledge about this vocation. As foster parents, we learn that we get back more than we give. Our rewards are seeing the differences we have made for our kids. My hope is that foster parents who read this book will know that their challenges have been experienced by many others who have gone before them.

I love the work that Allen and I continue to do with foster and adoptive parents. Through our seminars and workshops, we have met many extraordinary couples. We continue to have the opportunities to meet foster parents and share both our own and their experiences. For me, there is no greater group of people on this planet!

I hope that the information that was provided in this book will help foster parents continue the valuable work they do. In spite of the challenges that working in the foster care system presents, there are unique and wonderful people who will continue to make a difference in the lives of foster children. I wish all of you to feel the successes of your work and the knowledge and patience to overcome your obstacles.

Training Resources:

Foster Care and Adoptive Community: Provides on-line training for foster and adoptive parents. Among the 70 courses offered is a series entitled "Difficult Children" by Mary Goodearle with topics including: Difficult Children 101, Raising Foster and Adopted Teens, Foster Children With Post-Traumatic Stress, and Building on Their Resiliencies. Go to: www.fosterparents.com for more topics and information.

New Paradigms Unlimited: A company formed by Allen and Mary Goodearle with the mission of creating better environments for foster parents and children through their books, trainings, and seminars. For more information about topics and availability go to www.foster-caretrainer.com or email: newparadigms2000@yahoo.com.

References and Recommended Readings:

A Child's Journey Through Placement, by Vera I. Fahlberg, M.D.; Perspectives Press:1991.

Troubled Transplants, by Richard J. Delaney, Ph.D. and Frank R Kunstal, Ed.D.; University of Southern Maine: 1993.

Men Are From Mars, Women Are From Venus, by John Gray, PhD.; Quill Publishing: 2004.

Love Busters, by Willard F. Harley, Jr.; Baker Book House: 1992

Why Parents Disagree & What You Can Do About It, By Dr. Ron Taffel; Avon Parenting: 1994.

The 17 Essential Qualities of a Team Player, by John C. Maxwell; Thompson-Nelson Publishers: 2002.

The Wisdom of Teams, by Jon R. Katzenbach and Douglas K. Smith; Harper Collins Books: 1993.

Don't Sweat the Small Stuff, By Richard Carlson, Ph.D.: Hyperion Press: 1997

They Cage the Animals at Night, by Jennings Michael Burch; Signet Books: 1984

Get Out of My Life, by Anthony E. Wolf, Ph.D.; Harper Collins: 1991

Grounded for Life!, by Louise Felton Tracy, M.S.; Parenting Press 1994.

Recruitment and Retention of Foster Parents in Outagamie County, by Mary Goodearle; Thesis submitted to University of Wisconsin-Green Bay: 1995

ISBN 141207847-4

Made in the USA
San Bernardino, CA
14 May 2014